RELATIONSHIP
BREAKTHROUGH

RELATIONSHIP
BREAKTHROUGH

HOW TO CREATE
OUTSTANDING RELATIONSHIPS IN
EVERY AREA OF YOUR LIFE

CLOÉ MADANES

INTRODUCTION BY
TONY ROBBINS

RODALE

Library of Congress Cataloging-in-Publication Data
Madanes, Cloé
    Relationship breakthrough : how to create outstanding relationships in every area of your life / Cloé Madanes ; introduction by Tony Robbins.
        p.   cm.
    Includes bibliographical references and index.
    ISBN-13 978–1–60529–581–7 hardcover
    ISBN-10 1–60529–581–7 hardcover
  1. Interpersonal relations.   I. Title.
    HM1106.M33 2009
    158.2—dc22   2009029224

Distributed to the trade by Macmillan

2   4   6   8   10   9   7   5   3   1   hardcover

We inspire and enable people to improve their lives and the world around them
For more of our products visit **rodalestore.com** or call 800-848-4735

For Ingrid

CONTENTS

ACKNOWLEDGMENTS IX

FOREWORD BY TONY ROBBINS XI

INTRODUCTION BY CLOÉ MADANES XVII

PART I. UNDERSTANDING THE CHALLENGES IN OUR RELATIONSHIPS

1. What Are You Thinking? 3

2. Do You Know What You Really Need? 19

3. Your Model of the World 31

4. Triangles, Circles, and Who's on Top 49

5. Are You Really Saying What You Think You're Saying? 65

PART II. BREAKING THROUGH TO THE RELATIONSHIP YOU WANT

6. Be All of Who You Really Are 87

7. The Seven Master Steps of Relationship Breakthrough 101

8. Helplessness Is Powerful 121

9. Recovering from Loss 135

Conclusion: Breaking Through to Growth and Contribution 153

THE BREAKTHROUGH ALPHABET 155

THE WORKBOOK 161

END NOTES 215

BIBLIOGRAPHY 221

INDEX 227

ACKNOWLEDGMENTS

———————— //////////////////////////// ————————

Relationship Breakthrough grew out of my collaboration of 7 years with Tony Robbins and represents the integration of our thinking and our practice. Thank you, Tony, for your deep understanding of human nature, for your unswerving faith in the goodness of people, and for helping millions of people to create their own destiny. Thank you also for bouncing your ideas off of me, for listening to me patiently, and for putting up with me for all these years.

Many people contributed to this book. First of all, I want to thank all those who shared with me their most intimate relationship challenges and all the students and colleagues who helped to shape my ideas. My special thanks to Ann Patty, who gave shape to the book, and to Julie Will at Rodale, who meticulously went over the manuscript. I'm forever grateful to Jim Levine, who helped me every step of the way and who I'm certain is the best literary agent in the world.

The book is based, in great part, on the films and products that I made with Mark Peysha, my collaborator and son-in-law, about the work of Tony Robbins. Without his partnership, neither the films nor this book would ever have seen the light of day. Mark, I'm deeply grateful for your creativity, your persistence, your analytical mind, and for putting up with me over the years. Thank you also to my daughter, Magali Peysha, whose suggestions, critique, and support were invaluable in making this book possible.

Foreword by Tony Robbins

—————— *////////////////////////* ——————

Any time two people meet, a third world is formed that is like no other world. Together you create a different universe that's unlike any you've ever known. Appreciating and cherishing that world is what allows you to transform your life and your relationships.

Love has a spiritual quality that most of us only touch on a few times in our lives and very few people actually live. When we really love someone, there's a dynamic change that occurs within us: We stop focusing on ourselves. It's what people who strive to connect with God experience when they are in the deepest level of meditation. When you are in love with someone, the first thing that happens is that time disappears. Then you find that you need nothing else because you're getting exactly what you need. The third thing is that *you* disappear. It is not about you anymore. And that's when you experience your greatest joy.

But pretty soon, things change. You begin creating expectations about how your relationship *should* be. You try to bend this wild, unexplored spiritual territory to your will, trying to force it to fit your own expectations and requirements, instead of simply growing along with it. You start creating rules and measuring whether the love you're receiving is enough or not. In other words, it becomes all about you. And that's when love starts to die.

This has nothing to do with how long you've been together; it has to do with a pattern. Once you've developed a Belief System, you find a way to fulfill it. This happens not just in our most intimate relationships but also with our children, our friends, people at work. When you are connecting with others, you have a model for how they should be. If they don't match your model, you start questioning everything. Have I lied to myself? Have they said they love me but they don't? Are my expectations too high? Am I not beautiful enough? Successful enough? Smart enough? *Am I not enough?* These are the deep, internal questions that most people don't want to answer or answer too quickly and easily just to get closure.

What makes people so sad and depressed about their relationships is their learned helplessness. They don't know how to win. They start to win—they get so much juice and joy out of the love they receive—but then they begin to believe it doesn't last. It's *not* that it doesn't last. It's that they don't understand the dynamics of what creates that chemistry and keeps it alive.

For 3 decades I have been obsessed with answering the question *what makes people do what they do?* Why is it that so many of us say we want to serve, to love, to help somebody, we want a relationship, but every day we do either something that keeps us from moving forward or something that actually moves us in the opposite direction?

I've worked with millions of people in 100 different countries, helping them figure out who they really are, what they want their life to really represent, and where the meaning is for them. How do we learn from the life challenges we face and then master them? How do we end up on the other side, where we don't just protect our life, our identity, or our ego, but transcend what stops and limits us?

Here's your choice: Give up, live in fear, be pissed off at everybody else, run for cover, and live in anxiety—*or* do what's necessary to develop the muscle to live your life at the richest level you've ever dreamed of, in a place you never would have gotten to if these challenges had not shown up. The quality of your life comes down to one question: *How deep are you willing to go?*

All happiness comes from one word, *progress.* We grow or we die. There is no other choice, and life's problems and our relationships give us the biggest challenges to grow. Because nowhere else does our deepest fear show up: that we are not enough. To feel like we are worthless is to feel like we are dead psychologically, emotionally, and spiritually. I see this fear in action every day.

At my live seminars and workshops, I interact constantly with audience members—people who are suicidal, suffering from lifelong depression, facing a divorce or bankruptcy, people who have lost their children or spouses, or have been traumatized by rape or sexual abuse. In each case, I'm on the spot in the laboratory of life. As a practical psychologist, I've learned how to mobilize instantly and figure out what's really going on, what's stopping someone, what he or she needs, and how to create a shift.

Out of necessity I've had to find the triggers and tools that shift people's perception of what things mean and what they can do. I've developed techniques that can change not only their emotions and psychology, but also what actions they take to reshape their lives. And these aren't temporary changes—they last. We've done 2-, 3-, 4-, and 5-year follow-ups on these people. This doesn't mean they'll never face another challenge, but they never go back to that place where suicide is the only option.

Over the last 10 years, I've not only applied these cutting-edge techniques to transform the relationships in my own life but also had the privilege of sharing them with thousands of therapeutic professionals and coaches who are hungry for more, not only for their clients but for themselves as well. If you're going to transform someone else's inner game—the way they run their blueprint, which is their operating system, or shift their world view—do it on yourself first.

But I'm the kind of guy who's always looking to learn more, to make what I do for people more effective. So for years I'd been looking for someone I could learn from, too—someone whose work shows a new level of mastery in relationship dynamics. Frankly, after reading book after book, I had given up hope of finding any innovative, practical strategies that really made a measurable difference in people's lives. There were lots of empirical theories, but nothing was systematic and focused on core dynamics.

One day a friend handed me a book by a woman named Cloé Madanes, and *baboom!* I found myself reading it voraciously, underlining sentences on almost every page. Here was an approach that, like mine, honored the power of individual commitment and responsibility, and was also an action manual on navigating the paradoxes of interpersonal dynamics. Cloé had incredibly creative solutions to a host of relationship problems. Some of her suggestions were outrageously funny; others were simple and elegant.

I soon learned that Cloé is one of a handful of world-class experts in the field of interpersonal dynamics. Her books are considered classics, have been translated into more than 20 languages, and are taught in virtually every graduate-level class in family therapy. I wanted to learn from her and to show her the tools that I had developed, so I invited her to my home in Fiji to attend one of my programs. When she witnessed some of my interventions, she was fascinated.

As we began to share back and forth, magical things started to happen. I learned things from her that allowed me to do my work with even more potency. She expanded my world. And she felt that I expanded hers so much that we needed to begin working together.

We created the Robbins-Madanes Center for Strategic Intervention. We have synthesized our strategic approaches and developed a new school of psychology called Human Needs Psychology. This marvelous collaboration has led to a series of videos and products, such as the Ultimate Relationship Program. We are currently finishing an advanced training series that will enable professionals and laypeople alike to benefit from these valuable strategies.

We called this book **Relationship Breakthrough** because most people, at some point, feel stuck in the patterns of their relationships. Whatever your challenges are, this book will bring you to a place of clarity, insight, and results. Cloé has incorporated the best of both of our work and presents a cutting-edge method that makes it easier than ever to create deeply rewarding relationships that will sustain you for life.

In **Relationship Breakthrough** you'll learn how you can recapture, rekindle, or deepen love in any intimate relationship. We'll show you how to communicate with your spouse, children, and others in ways that invigorate and motivate them to take positive action. You'll also find ways to resolve long-standing, persistent conflicts between family members simply by making a change within yourself.

For example, how many times have you found yourself trying to share something from your heart or get something done, and you get this push-back, this resistance, from the other person? Say that you're a driven, successful executive, and your son spends all his time watching clips on YouTube or playing video games. Odds are that he has made his choices in reaction to the choices you've made, which is why he's become immune to your advice over time. You don't understand what's driving him—his model of the world. You're trying to influence him through yours, but it never seems to work. What's ironic is that the more you react, the more you express your frustration, and the more you're playing right into his game.

So what do you do? The first step is to appreciate the dynamics of the relationship that's so challenging for you. It isn't that your son is being willful to you or ignoring you. It's not that you're incompetent or impotent to create change. It's that you don't understand the system that's in operation. Next, *you* change. If I want to change your behavior, the first thing I've got to do is change my own. The blueprint that says you're wrong and I'm right—if I can just get you to understand the way it's supposed to be (i.e., my world view) and get you to follow it, then we'll both be happy—is not only ignorant but futile.

We'll show you the limits of your own model of the world, your own beliefs, your own conditions, your own path—and the opportunities for change and expansion that will revitalize any relationship you are in, intimate or otherwise. There's also the awe and love of being able to dig inside someone, understand his model of the world and all the rules he has about being with you. It's part of the game you set up together unconsciously.

We're not just going to give you principles; you're going to be reading the transcripts of live interactions and living these transformational moments. If you want to experience this more intensely, go online and watch one of our introductory videos so you can see people's facial expressions and the emotions they're moving through during the process.

My wish is that this book will help accelerate not only your understanding but also your appreciation of your own life, and that you'll be able to convey this to someone else because you've experienced the value yourself. I also hope you will come to know yourself and those around you at such a level of depth that you can either transform the most important relationship in your life or find the one you desire and deserve.

I believe no matter what else you accomplish in your life, if you're not happy with your relationships, you're not going to be happy. I'm talking here from personal experience. Despite many challenges, I'm living the most amazing life anybody could hope for, but there's nothing I would trade on this earth for the relationship I have with Sage, my wife. I thank God because she is the greatest gift He's given me. Sage has helped me so much through her appreciation and understanding, courage, loyalty, and love.

It wasn't my prowess or luck that brought this beautiful soul into my life. It was my vulnerability and my willingness to ask questions that I didn't want to ask about myself and others and to pursue the greater spirit within myself to serve something more than myself. It's my decision to dive deeply into myself that's given me this gift.

Knowledge is not power—it's potential power. Knowledge that you apply with heart, that's real power. That's what you'll bring to the table after you understand the dynamics of your relationships. We'd love to hear from you about your experiences using these strategies and your thoughts on how they might help others. You are welcome to communicate through our Web site or through e-mail.

I'm confident that the words that follow will start you on that journey with more momentum than you'd ever imagined possible, simply because it's based on real-life experiences with real people. Let the journey begin.

With love, respect, and passion,
Anthony Robbins

INTRODUCTION

I have taught several generations of psychotherapists around the world how to help couples and families. I have always believed that quick, dramatic change for the better is possible for anyone. The human spirit has the capacity to triumph in the face of all kinds of adversity. Relationships have the power to heal.

We all confront challenges in our relationships. Whether with spouses, lovers, partners, children, parents, friends, or co-workers, relationships have the power to make us happy or intensely miserable. This book explains how to truly understand how we relate to each other and what we need to know to create and sustain outstanding relationships.

The reader of this book is a wife or a husband interested in a happy marriage; a professional who wants to better understand her clients; an executive who needs to relate better to a business partner; parents who wish to relate better to their children and to teach them how to relate to others; adult children who need to deal with difficult parents; single people who want to find love that is reciprocated; and teachers who want to help students to be smart about their relationships.

With this book, I am reaching out to readers who are not trained in any of the helping professions, and making the knowledge I have gained as a professional over many years available to everyone.

I believe in free will, but I also believe that each of us is embedded in a system of relationships that has a mind of its own. That is, each of us is a free spirit with infinite possibilities, yet we all live under the constraints of the relationships with those we love and those we need to collaborate with. This book will elucidate some of the traps we fall into when we negotiate the space between our free will and our relationships. We all have our own personalities and points of view, but the moment we become part of something bigger—a relationship—that entity takes on its own "personality" with its own dynamic and "rules."

However, we all have much more freedom of choice than we imagine. Although it's true that our childhood, our social context, and our biology influence us, there is always a choice to be made. When Viktor Frankl was a prisoner at Auschwitz, he chose to write a book. The book was seized by the Nazis, and he wrote it again. That book, *Man's Search for Meaning*, has influenced generations of therapists. Frankl had a choice in the concentration camp: He could succumb to despair, he could commit suicide, or he could write a book. He chose to write a book. There are always choices. For most of us, our range of choices is greatly influenced by our most important relationships. That is why it is essential to create and plan our relationships carefully. Relationships don't just happen to us—even with family, to some degree, we choose the kind of relationship (close, friendly, formal, and so forth) that we have with them. The people with whom we choose to be in relationships and the kind of relationships we choose to create or take part in are some of the biggest decisions we make in life.

Our relationships define who we are. No one lives in isolation. An individual is not just an individual, but a part of a couple; a couple is not just a couple, but part of a family; and a family is not just a family, but part of a community. This book will show you how to understand your relationships and give you step-by-step tools to vastly improve them.

We exist insofar as we relate to one another. What defines us as human is our need to relate, to be accepted, and to be confirmed in our reality. When two people communicate, they create a sphere, a field of endeavor that is common to them but that reaches out beyond their interaction. The "yes" from a friend, the look of a lover, the emotions we feel as we think about someone, these are what liberate us from our fear of being alone, of abandonment, and of death.

We suffer most in our lives from failed or failing relationships—marital strife, parental rejection, difficulties with friends—or from the lack of relationships—isolation, alienation, erosion of community. Any contribution to the process of achieving happiness and avoiding suffering must focus on improving our relationships. We live in a world of possibilities and constraints, and it is my hope that this book will bring some equilibrium and harmony to your relationships and so contribute to the art of living.

In this book you will learn how to understand your relationship with your partner, your children, your colleagues, your friends. I will also give you tools for change and show you how to increase passion—not just sexual or erotic passion, but vitality, enthusiasm, joy. We have all had the experience of thinking that we truly understand another person. If the model we have constructed of the person we live with has served us well for some time, we tend to believe that we know who that person really is. But sooner or later our companion does something unexpected. It can be shocking, and we might initially think that the person has changed, but that's rarely the case. The other person has merely shown an aspect we had not incorporated into our model, because no prior situation had brought it to our attention. The other we know is not the other as he or she is, but a model we have constructed on the basis of our own experience. We tell ourselves stories about who we are and who other people are—stories that are constructed through our own points of view and the way we see the world and our relationships. When the other person doesn't fit our story, we can be shocked, disappointed, and angry, questioning whether we ever truly knew this person.

The same thing happens to our model of, for instance, the planetary system or the universe. When a model works well and provides useful answers, it comes to be considered as a true description of reality. But sooner or later something incompatible is observed, a recession of Mercury or a beam of light that does not follow a straight line. Such observations constitute *constraints* that no longer fit the accepted model and that make it unviable. Eventually a new model is constructed that fits the new observations. This book will provide new models for understanding relationships and new strategies for improving them.

This book integrates Tony Robbins's work, ideology, and technology with my ideas, my values, and my strategies for transforming people and healing relationships. Both Tony Robbins and I are indebted to Dr. Milton Erickson, from whose work many of the ideas in this book evolved. He is probably the most influential American psychiatrist and hypnotist and a master of metaphorical communication and indirect influence. He developed the most sophisticated techniques for leading people to see their choices and to make changes in their lives. Several schools of therapy developed from his work. Both Tony Robbins and I were greatly influenced by his subtle examples of breaking negative patterns in relationships and creating new unexpected possibilities. Severely dyslexic and confined to a wheelchair for most of his life after contracting polio, Erickson was the epitome of the American can-do spirit. I was his patient for a few days many years ago when I was having trouble overcoming the grief over my father's sudden death. To this day I don't know what he was doing when he talked to me, but I came out of those conversations overcoming my grief and focused on the contribution I was going to make to the field of psychology. Erickson was known for helping women to fulfill their dreams in the days when many women encountered great obstacles.

A good part of this book is dedicated to explaining what Tony Robbins actually does to transform the audience at his events that draw thousands of people, through his audio programs that have helped millions of people, and when he coaches individuals—entrepreneurs, world leaders, and famous artists and athletes.

This book makes accessible to everyone Robbins's skills in transforming the lives of millions of people, together with my expertise in creating healing, empowering relationships. This book is filled with simple step-by-step procedures and examples to help you understand whomever you are interacting with as well as to understand yourself; to connect with others; to resolve conflicts; and to create outstanding relationships in every area of your life. In the Workbook section at the back of this book, you will find exercises designed to help you put these relationship skills into practice.

Some of my objectives are:

- To encourage you to deliberately and purposefully control your behavior, rather than be controlled by others or by uncontrollable impulses.

- To encourage you to recognize that you are not passive, that you are in control of your body *and* mind, so that you are not subject to unpleasant or unproductive thinking. I want you to feel empowered by this recognition.

- To help you control violence and anger—of all the actions and emotions to be controlled, these are the most important.

- To develop your empathy so you can be more intelligent and fair in relationships. This book will help you to gain a more accurate understanding of someone else's point of view and, ultimately, to better understand human nature and human suffering. This will enable you to be a better relationship partner and a more compassionate, kinder person.

- To encourage hope (a situation can only be resolved if it is not seen as hopeless) and humor (which is what makes the human condition bearable).

- To promote tolerance and compassion so that you can live within your family and your community.
- To encourage forgiveness and kindness as the only ways to live in relationships.
- To promote harmony and balance within you as an individual and in your relationships.
- To harness and direct your enthusiasm for what is truly important.

It is my hope that this book will provide enlightenment and rekindle the light of all those who seek greater happiness through love and improved relationships.

Cloé Madanes
La Jolla, California

PART I

UNDERSTANDING THE CHALLENGES IN OUR RELATIONSHIPS

Chapter 1

WHAT ARE YOU THINKING?

Not much in life compares with the feeling of being a *We*, not just an *I*, of giving and receiving love freely, of being part of a team. The varieties of such relationships are legion: between spouses, lovers, parents and children, siblings, relatives, intimate friends, co-workers, neighbors. It is the feeling we get when we know someone is helping us "pull the wagon" in an endeavor, when someone "has our back." There is immense joy in a happy, permanent relationship. Most of us want nothing more than a permanent bond with someone we love. Yet so often our relationships go bad, and we don't know how to turn them around.

We all want the perfect relationship; alas, there is no such thing. Relationships are messy. It's how we deal with the messiness that makes the difference between a relationship filled with passion, growth, depth, and joy, and one that is mired in negative patterns of anger, blame, and boredom. A good relationship—whether with a partner, child, friend, or family member—is one of life's greatest gifts, and there's no reason to settle for anything less. When problems and conflicts arise, I counsel against exchanging one relationship for another, like a Christmas gift we take back for a store credit in hope of finding that thing we desire most. I believe most troubled relationships can be transformed into satisfying, rewarding ones. Simply falling into a great, long-lasting relationship is about as rare as finding a gold coin on the street. Good relationships take work, but we all

3

have the capacity to create joyful, lasting, deeply satisfying connections in our lives.

Relationships are not always what they appear to be. A submissive wife may actually dominate her husband, even though he is the one who appears dominating. A loving husband may only get angry responses from his wife—could his loving behavior possibly be the cause of her anger? How do we understand cause and effect in relationships? What are the sources of power that one person has over another? When we overcome a challenge, are we creating new problems? Is it possible to plan what will happen in relationships?

The first step to changing a dysfunctional or unsatisfying relationship is to change our focus—to look underneath the obvious problem and focus on our underlying needs.

It's Likely You Created the Problem
You Are Trying to Solve

It is human nature that when faced with difficulties in a relationship, we tend to blame the other person.

> "If my husband were not so rigid in his views about everything, then we could communicate. He becomes judgmental even before I can express myself!"

> "I walk on eggshells around my son for fear that anything I might say could produce an emotional outburst!"

> "He is so critical of everything I do! I am never good enough for him."

> "Her hostility is out of control. The moment she opens her mouth, I expect to be attacked."

> "He wants me to do everything for him, just like his mother did."

These are common complaints in relationships. They could have been expressed by a spouse about the other spouse, by a parent about a child, or by a child about a parent. The typical belief is that if only the other person would change, the relationship would be much better. And so people get stuck in patterns of blaming one another.

Most of us see ourselves as innocent bystanders in our relationships. The way we are seems totally unrelated to how others behave. Reality, of course, is quite different. We tend to only see things from our own point of view. We tell ourselves a story about "us," and this story can be very different from reality. Even though we prefer to deny it, we know that in relationships everything is interaction and that our behavior provokes a response in the other and that response in turn provokes a reaction and so on.

For example, if a wife expresses an outrageous view, the husband might respond with a cautious, conservative opinion, which she will then criticize, and he will respond by becoming even more rigid in his view. It's often difficult to determine what came first—her outrageousness or his rigidity.

Wife: I'm going to get the new Volkswagen Rabbit. I love the shape and the colors!

Husband: We need to look at the safety and consumer ratings before we make a decision.

Wife: You're so boring! Buying a car is like buying a dress; it's the shape and the color that matter.

Husband: We are not buying a new car this year. We simply can't afford it.

In every situation, we make three unconscious decisions: what we focus on, what it means to us, and what we should do to create the results we desire. While the wife was focusing on the pleasing aesthetics of the car, the husband was focusing on safety and performance ratings and finances. By changing her mental framework, her point of view, the wife might have changed her husband's reactions. If she had taken into account the sorts of concerns she knew her husband would focus on, she might have presented her desire differently.

If the wife had said, "I'm thinking of getting the new Volkswagen Rabbit. I love the shape and the colors, and I think it has great ratings," the husband's response might have been different. Likewise if the husband had replied to her first statement with "I like the shape and the colors, too. Let's look up the ratings," the wife might not have immediately jumped to the conclusion that her husband was boring.

A simple change of focus can immediately change a habitual mode of conflict.

Attempted Solutions May Sustain
a Problem Instead of Resolving It

Sigmund Freud observed that people tend to repeat the same behaviors over and over again, even when those behaviors make them unhappy. He was interested in how people make the same mistake repeatedly, even when knowing that they are making a mistake. For example, a woman falls in love with a man, and soon she becomes emotionally dependent on him and demanding. He feels stifled and leaves her. She then falls in love with another man. Again she becomes dependent and demanding, again he leaves her. Freud called this the repetition compulsion.

Charles Darwin had already observed that the survival of a species might be threatened by its inability to abandon what at one time was an optimal adaptation. When a creature stubbornly maintains the same behavior in the face of a changing environment, survival is at risk. Yet changing habitual patterns can be very difficult to do, as everyone knows who has tried to abandon a bad habit or get someone else to do so.

Every marital therapist has struggled with spouses who think they have an optimal solution to their spouse's bad behavior. A typical issue for wives is the husband's sloppiness. The idea that husbands are sloppy might sound like a stereotype, but I reference it because often it is a problem in many relationships.

A conversation might go like this:

Wife: I get upset and yell at my husband when he leaves a mess in the kitchen.

Therapist: Does yelling work, or does he do it again?

Wife: He does it again.

Therapist: So then what do you do?

Wife: I yell louder.

Therapist: Does it work?

Wife: No.

Therapist: Perhaps it's time to stop doing what doesn't work and try something different.

It's remarkable how difficult it is to abandon an attempted solution that we believe will work, but time and time again doesn't. Not only is the solution not abandoned; it is often intensified or embellished. By attempting to perfect the solution, we can become blind to other strategies for change that may be available to us at any time. And to change, we need to shake up our old patterns of behavior, to think out of the box.

The inability to change the way we attempt to solve a problem can prove to be fatal to a relationship, even to a life. For example, army ants (*Eciton*) are known to have an almost unbelievably complex and purposeful social order. They march in columns of thousands and are extremely aggressive. However, an ironic disaster occasionally overcomes them when they are marching. A rainfall can wash away all traces of their colony trail. Having lost the trail, they begin to follow in each other's footsteps, and pretty soon they are walking in a dense circle that can involve thousands of ants—and they continue to walk in this ever-compacting circle until they die. Apparently, they have only one solution to attempt when they lose their trail, and that is to follow each other, even though this solution eventually kills them.[1]

Attempted solutions that don't work and that actually exacerbate problems are as commonplace in the physical world as they are in our social world of relationships. In medicine they are so frequent that there is even a name for illnesses caused by a doctor's attempts to cure another illness. They are called iatrogenic.[2] In many of our relationships, our attempted solutions become chronic as we repeat over and over a strategy that doesn't work, and we become like the ants, marching endlessly around and around, getting nowhere. Just as with bad habits, when we repeat certain behaviors, they become second nature, even when they're not good for us.

Sometimes Our Attempted Solution Becomes Bigger Than the Problem We Want to Solve

Let's say Jerry is a slob. He drops his clothes wherever he takes them off, leaving a trail of dirty clothes around the house. His wife, Eva, over the years, has become more and more annoyed by the habit. She's sick of picking up after him. But no matter how much she nags, Jerry can't seem to remember not to simply leave his clothes where they fall. Every day she comments on the dirty socks in front of the couch, yesterday's shirt on the bedroom floor, yesterday's underwear on the floor by the shower: "Pick up your socks. I'm sick of coming out every morning and seeing your smelly old socks in front of the couch. Why can't you put them in the laundry before you go to bed?" "Your shirts are on the floor again." "I can't stand the mess you leave in the bathroom," and so on. Every day Jerry answers: "In a minute." "Okay." "Sorry." He does as he has been ordered, but only after she nags him. Over time the interchange becomes almost ritualistic. She complains, he apologizes and eventually does as he is told. The problem is no longer simply that he doesn't pick up his clothes. The problem has become the unpleasant interaction around picking up the clothes, which leaves Jerry feeling harassed, unappreciated, and nagged, and Eva feeling frustrated and angry and as if Jerry doesn't care how his behavior affects her.

What if Eva changed her attempted solution and tried something completely different? Instead of complaining or pointing out the clothes Jerry has left all over the house, she might passionately kiss him every time she sees that he has picked up an item of clothing—even if he's picked it up only to put it on again. Without uttering a word, she kisses him. Jerry is puzzled as to why the sudden passion, but after a few incidents, he sees that there are large rewards for the small effort of picking up his socks.

You might think that a woman should not have to kiss her husband when he's being disrespectful to her. You might think: "Why would I be in the mood to kiss someone who can't pick up after himself?" That is precisely the issue. From the point of view of the story Eva tells herself, Jerry is being disrespectful to her by not picking up his socks. From Jerry's point of view, he is simply taking off his socks; he's not thinking that Eva will pick them up later. However, Jerry's behavior can easily be changed when the story is no longer about disrespect but is about playfulness and passion.

This was actually an experiment conducted as part of a doctoral dissertation. A number of wives of graduate students had the same complaint: The husbands didn't pick up their clothes no matter how much the wives complained, nagged, and cajoled them. The experimenter instructed the women to stop all those behaviors, and instead each would kiss her husband passionately whenever he happened to pick up a clothing item. In a matter of weeks, all the husbands were regularly picking up their clothes.

By adding a dimension of surprise, spontaneity, and playfulness, the wife has changed not only her focus (I *want* that man to pick up those clothes, I'm not going to do it for him this time) but also her husband's (All I have to do is clean up a bit and she's in the mood—oops, there are some socks on the floor, let me pick them up, I think she may be watching me out of the corner of her eye).

Positive reinforcement is always more effective than negative.

Change the Solution

I have worked with many couples in which the husbands complained that their wives wouldn't stop talking about unpleasant matters. The issue could be money, in-laws, the children, or the relatives. At dinner together, on a walk, during a visit with friends, even on vacation, the wives would bring up the same old issues. They wanted to be heard. Being heard made them feel understood and loved. But the husbands were overwhelmed by the negativity that seemed to permeate every interaction. They were unable to divert their wives' focus onto some other more pleasant subject of conversation.

I suggested that the husbands propose to arrange for a meeting once a week where the couple would be able to discuss these unpleasant issues, with the explicit instruction that at no other time should they discuss these matters unless it was an absolute emergency. Once the couple had agreed to this, the husband was told, in the presence of his wife, that should she forget the instructions and begin to discuss one of these matters outside of the special meeting, he should begin to take off his clothes. He might first remove his tie, then his watch, his shoes, his socks, and continue undressing no matter where they were, for as long as the wife continued to talk about the issues. He will continue to undress even if it means that he will end up naked in public. The husbands typically loved this idea, and the wives quickly learned to remember to stay away from stressful subjects when the couple is having a good time together.

Sound outrageous? That's the point—we have to move out of our zone of comfort, which so often involves destructive patterns, and into our zone of creative power. This might seem extreme, but the point is that we need to find a way to break the pattern of negative interactions and turn them into playful exchanges. Introducing outrageous behavior and humor is a great way of doing this.

If we create the problems we struggle to solve, then it follows logically that by changing our focus we can create interesting challenges that resolve the problem along the way.

Creating Good Memories

Bob and Sally came to therapy with a serious problem. Sally was diabetic and was drinking herself to death. She drank a half bottle of vodka a night and was not paying attention to her diet or her medications. She said she had to drink because of the pain of her bad relationship with her husband. Both she and Bob were tall and overweight. Bob was ill-tempered; he had never laid a hand on Sally, but he was known to smash a plate of spaghetti against the wall when he got in a rage. Sally sometimes came to the sessions wearing shorts and curlers in her hair, which was something that I had not seen in many years. Bob and Sally quarreled endlessly about messes: the attic, the garage, cleaning up after the dog, taking out the garbage.

Their therapist was a nice young man, always dressed in a suit and a tie, and I was his supervisor, observing behind a one-way mirror. I could see that as Steve struggled to help this couple—and the couple was not getting any better—Steve was getting more and more depressed. They were the kind of people that make the most dedicated of therapists think, "For this I struggled through a PhD program?"

One day I said to Steve, "Today I would like you to ask Sally whether she has seen the movie or read the book *Gone with the Wind*. When she wants to know why you are asking, I want you to tell her that she and her husband remind you so much of Rhett Butler and Scarlett O'Hara. They have the same kind of passionate relationship—always fighting. Like Rhett, Bob is always on the verge of violence. Scarlett was always trying to change Rhett; tell them that it's curious to you that Sally continues to try to change Bob, instead of enjoying his passionate nature, when even Scarlett couldn't change Rhett."

Steve liked this idea. As he began to talk to Sally, Bob, whose only resemblance to Clark Gable was that he wore a moustache, began to stroke it.

Sally was delighted at being compared to Vivien Leigh. By fortuitous coincidence, Sally was an expert on *Gone with the Wind*. She had seen the movie six times and read the book twice. She immediately said, "Scarlett did change Rhett!" Steve responded, "I bet you 10 dollars that you don't find one line in the book that says that Rhett changed one bit from the beginning to the end of the novel."

Sally took the challenge and eventually conceded that Steve was right; Rhett had not changed at all.

The comparison with Scarlett and Rhett had set the tone for another type of interaction between Sally and Bob. How could they continue talking about messes when they had just been compared to the most romantic couple of the Western world? Steve had raised them to a higher level of being.

Once they were at this level, instead of focusing on messes, alcohol, illness, or medications, Steve said, "I want you to tell me what are the best memories that you have of your life together. Something that happened during your courtship, your honeymoon, something related to the children—your best memories."

Immediately both Bob and Sally said that they didn't have any good memories. They had always quarreled and said nasty things to each other. Steve insisted that every couple has *some* good memories, and he asked them to just sit quietly thinking so that some good memories would come back.

After a few minutes, Bob said that he remembered something. They had gone to Florida for their honeymoon. One evening Bob went for a walk by himself to a lagoon where a trainer was working with dolphins. He learned the signals that the trainer gave the dolphins, and the next evening he took Sally for a walk, gave the signals to the dolphins, and they put on a show just for her.

As Sally remembered this incident, she was moved and looked at Bob fondly. Then she remembered another wonderful thing that Bob had done on the birth of their first child. So now they had two good memories.

Steve told them that in the next 2 weeks, before he saw them again, he wanted them to do one special thing and that was to create a good memory together. He said, "The quarrels about the dog and the garbage are something that 10 or 20 years from now you will not remember. But if you create an extraordinary memory like the one about the dolphins, that is something that you will have to treasure forever."

That day was the first snow of the winter. When the couple left the session, Bob built a big snowman, right at the door of our Institute, which is something that we will always remember.

For 3 months, Bob and Sally came to see Steve every 2 weeks. Each time they told him about the good memory they had created, and each time they planned the good memory that they would create next. They didn't have much money, so they had to be creative and resourceful in finding wonderful things to do with each other and with their children.

During those 3 months, Sally quit drinking and her health improved as she began to take care of herself. She said she could do that because now she was having such a good time with Bob and they were so happy together.

Therapy was no longer necessary, and they brought their children to meet Steve before they said good-bye.

The focus on the positive fact that Bob and Sally were capable of creating wonderful memories diverted them from their negativity. As they were able to bring out the best in themselves, they were also able to bring out the best in each other. We should all live by the idea of creating good memories with those we love.

Let's say you and your spouse are struggling with a lack of passion and enthusiasm in your relationship. Invent a new issue. Focus, for example, on what fun it would be to learn to fly and plan the details of when, where, and how to save the money to be able to do it. Or talk about how next year you could get tickets for the Super Bowl or vacation in Mexico. You have created a new challenge that can be solved, and, as you solve it, you might find that the old problem will go away. When we change our focus from the negative to the positive, we change our story and our point of view, and we discover new aspects about ourselves and about each other.[3]

The Plan for Our Relationships

It is difficult for some people to accept the idea that we deliberately plan how to influence our significant relationships. Yet it is impossible not to acknowledge that we do. As soon as we ask *to what end* a person behaves in that way, instead of asking *why* someone behaves in a certain way, it becomes apparent that a person's actions are related to a change they desire to bring about.

Even parts of our anatomy are surprisingly receptive to our influence and the influence of others. Here is an example of an experiment done on warts. A wart is the "elaborate reproductive apparatus of a virus," says Lewis Thomas. It is a tough overgrowth in which viruses flourish. Yet warts can be ordered off the skin by hypnotic suggestion, even though currently it is thought that there are complex immunological mechanisms implicated in the rejection of warts. The renowned physician, scientist, and writer Lewis Thomas, in his classic book *The Medusa and the Snail*,[4] marvels at the ability of the unconscious, which can "manipulate the mechanisms needed for getting around that virus, and for deploying all the various cells in the correct order for tissue rejection." He points out that, even if immunology is not involved, if all that happens is that the blood supply to the warts is shut off, this is a tremendous task.

If we had a clear understanding of what goes on when a wart is hypnotized away, "we would be finding out about a kind of super intelligence that exists in each of us, infinitely smarter and possessed of technical know-how far beyond our present understanding." Thomas seems to assume that the owner of the wart makes it go away—that the hypnotist tells the "unconscious" of the subject to make the wart disappear, and the unconscious does it. Yet it is the hypnotist who makes the wart go away. If we could understand the interaction between the hypnotist and the virus lodged in another person's skin, we would know infinitely more about the influence that people have over one another. If it is possible that one person can influence another so that the subtle and complex mechanisms necessary to eliminate warts will take place, what other kinds of influence are possible?

A successful career woman may be married to a man who has not found success in his career. She cannot help her husband in his work, but she can make him feel that he is essential to her. She might develop a problem—depression, anxiety, or a phobia. Her husband becomes her support and helper and begins to see himself as the more competent person in the marriage—now he is needed and stronger than his wife. A difference in status between partners can create such feelings of inferiority in a relationship that the wife developing a problem, thus raising her husband's sense of self-esteem, can save a faltering relationship. A father comes home from work upset and angry with his boss. He is ready to take out his rage on his wife. As soon as he begins to engage with her in a way that will lead to violence, the older son hits his little brother. The father turns to the older son in rage and hits him. The mother has been spared. Is it possible that the boy deliberately planned his behavior in order to protect the mother from the father's anger? Or was it the mother who somehow provoked or directed her older son to hit the younger brother so she would be spared? Could it be that all three, or even all four, family members planned this interaction?

It may seem difficult to conceive that a child could plan the reaction of others to his behavior, but it is even more difficult to conceive that he doesn't. Children are capable of planning complex systems of interaction. Children do have that intelligence and so do most creatures. Here's another example from Lewis Thomas's (1980) description of a beetle, the "mimosa girdler."[5]

The mimosa girdler showed Thomas that a creature without a true central nervous system could plan ahead. The beetle lives only on mimosa trees. She selects a limb, crawls out a short distance, and uses her mandible to cut a slit in the limb. Then she lays her eggs there. The slit heals very quickly, so the eggs can't be seen. She then climbs back toward the trunk of the tree and digs a girdle around the limb that holds her eggs—a girdle just deep enough to kill the limb. Sooner or later, the limb dies and breaks off; now the larvae are in dead wood, where they can hatch. This cycle repeats itself generation after generation. Lewis marvels that evolution achieved these two separate and unrelated acts of behavior. "It looks as though it's really been thought out. She wants to lay her eggs in the mimosa because it is somehow attractive. They can't live in live wood, and the nicest way to kill the wood is to girdle it."

What might be the complexities and mysteries of the ways humans plan ahead if the little beetle does it with such sophistication! The beetle has a plan, but she cannot help having a plan; she cannot stop following the plan. It may well be that the child helps the parents or that the wife helps the husband, but neither can stop helping. Sometimes the wife and the child express that they act deliberately. The wife might say, "When I'm depressed, my husband feels important and gives me affection." The child may say, "I knew my father was going to hit my mother and hurt her, but when he hits me he doesn't hurt me so much." Spouses and children have been known to say these things. They might have the illusion that they are acting deliberately, but in fact they may be part of a system with a purpose larger than their own.

A New Approach: Human Needs Psychology

Often we become so focused on a habitual conflict in a relationship that we fail to see what the conflict is really about. Most often, the conflict is not the cause of our dissatisfaction, but the result of our needs not being met in our relationship. When we change our focus, we discover our power to change.

We all have needs, desires, motivations, and strategies for getting along in life. We all live in relationships, to family, spouses, significant others, friends, co-workers. And it is where our needs, desires, motivations, and strategies are out of sync with our relationships that trouble brews. A daughter's greatest need may be to be loved by her father, who is too busy to demonstrate his love. A husband's greatest desire might be to see his wife happy, but she may be too preoccupied with her son's difficulties. A person's most important motivation may be to feel secure at work, but difficult economic times may make this impossible. These are just some examples of how what we crave most may be out of sync with our relationships and our social context.

From the beginning, psychology has tried to understand what makes us who we are, and how we might live more satisfying lives and create more lasting, loving relationships. Even though we see examples all around us of how people can change, often quickly and radically, the prevailing view in psychology has been that human beings are predetermined by forces outside their control.

First, there was Freud's concept of basic drives or instincts that predetermine our lives. Then came the concept of our parents as creators. We are what our parents have made us to be, products of our childhood experiences. Each individual is seen as the result of a faulty production process.

Then came the concept of the individual as an amalgam of chemistry and genetics. Here, too, the human being is seen as a predetermined object. The physician steps in to change moods and thought processes by chemical means.

An old but recently revamped concept is attachment disorder. We are determined by how our parents allowed us to attach to them in early childhood. Those original attachments allegedly determine our brain chemistry and our possibilities in life. Even though new positive attachments may correct our defective brain circuits, when things go wrong in the present, our early attachment disorders are to blame.

With systems thinking, another view of human beings as predetermined objects developed. The individual is seen as the product of a social context. The organization determines the existence of each of its members. The family, the school, the workplace are the creators, and each individual is part of the whole self-regulatory mechanism.

Many systemic thinkers were attracted to this concept because they wanted to escape from ideas of the individual being predetermined from without, by bad parents, bad attachments, and bad chemistry, only to find themselves mired in yet another concept that results in the individual not having responsibility for himself.

In spite of all these theories, it remains a well-known fact that a person is what she conceives herself to be. Everyone knows that some people who were abused, tortured, and suffered horrible hardships became loving, dedicated members of society, while others, raised by loving, giving parents became criminals. We are what we make of our circumstances.

In human needs psychology, we believe each individual is a self-determined entity. We believe an individual is a subject that acts, not an object that is acted upon.

Respect for each individual's self-determination is the first principle of human needs psychology. Responsibility is always personal responsibility.

This doesn't mean that there is no difference between the rich and the poor, the oppressor and the oppressed. On the contrary, the oppressor and the rich have more possibilities to choose. Human needs psychology cannot be used to justify social injustice. On the contrary, we seek to increase the range of choices of each individual person.

Choice is action. Compassion only exists in the compassionate deed; violence only exists in the violent act; love is only present in the loving gesture.

Our approach to relationships does not allow a person to explain, rationalize, or justify his acts as the fault or doing of something (pathology, syndrome, or person) stronger than himself.

We encourage individuals to face the fact that they are what they have chosen to be and that they can change or modify the choices they have made. We can always make new, different choices.

We do not label people with one syndrome or another, thus robbing them of personal responsibility, freedom, and respect for themselves and for others.

We recognize the paradoxes of life and the sense of humor that comes with that recognition.

We believe that no matter what the circumstances, we have a choice as to what to make of ourselves and our circumstances. Biology, chemistry, early attachments, the family, and the social context are influences that each one of us can choose or refuse to be affected by.

We recognize that self-determination is a heavy burden. Difficult choices can best be tolerated when a person has a goal, a purpose in life that transcends his or her own self.

We believe that not acting is itself an action.

We encourage everyone to be courageous and to think out of the box.

It is through these principles that we work with relationships. The underlying purpose of all our important relationships is to meet our needs and the needs of our significant others. In any relationship you must understand the other person's needs, as well as your own needs, in order to know what's really going on. If you know your partner's needs, you can avoid the frustration and disappointment that come from the feeling that you are "giving them everything" when, in fact, you may be giving them everything *except* what they really need. Knowing what the other person really needs not only wards off potential conflict but also opens up a whole new world of intimacy and understanding between two people. It means understanding someone you care about at a different level—knowing what motivates them, what frightens them, and what is meaningful to them.

Most of us have needs that are very specific, like a "secret button" that will trigger our feelings of love, connection, and gratitude. If you can discover what needs your loved one values most and how he satisfies those needs, you'll know how to satisfy him.

Chapter 2

DO YOU KNOW WHAT YOU REALLY NEED?

All of us have basic needs, not merely desires but profound needs that underlie and motivate every choice we make. There are six basic needs that everyone seeks to fulfill.[1]

Certainty/Comfort

The first need is for certainty. We want to feel safe, avoid pain, and feel comfortable in our environment and our relationships. Every individual needs to have some sense of certainty and security—a roof over one's head, knowing where the next meal will come from, knowing how to obtain care when one is sick, knowing that a neighbor won't attack us. These are just a few examples of what constitutes a basic sense of certainty.

The helpless infant needs certainty as well as the child, the adult, and the elderly person. The degree to which certainty is needed or desired, however, varies from person to person. Some people feel secure living in one room and collecting an unemployment check. Others can feel certainty only if they make a million dollars each year. Even though some certainty is necessary to all of us, what constitutes certainty varies from individual to individual. Code words for certainty are *comfort, security, safety, stability, feeling grounded, predictability,* and *protection.*

Uncertainty/Variety

The second need is for uncertainty—for variety and challenges that will exercise our emotional and physical range. Everyone needs some variety in life. Our bodies, our minds, our emotional well-being all require uncertainty, exercise, suspense, surprise.

The person caught in the same routine day after day will seek change and look for uncertainty. Just as a sense of security is reassuring, so the excitement that comes from variety is necessary to feel alive. For some, variety may be satisfied by watching the news on television. Others may seek extreme high-risk activities such as extreme sports or compulsive sexuality to satisfy the need for uncertainty. For many, a major source of variety is to experience problems. Code words for uncertainty/variety are *fear, instability, change, chaos, entertainment, suspense, exertion, surprise, conflict,* and *crisis.*

Significance

The third need is for significance. Every person needs to feel important, needed, wanted. As babies, we all needed to feel that we were number one. Children in a family compete with each other and find a way to be special, to feel unique. Significance comes from comparing ourselves to others—in our quest for significance, we are always involved in hierarchical pecking orders and questions of superiority or inferiority. We can feel significant because we have achieved something, built something, succeeded at something, or we can seek significance by tearing down something or somebody.

In its positive aspect, significance leads us to raise our standards. But if we are overly focused on significance, we will have trouble truly connecting with others—comparisons focus on differences rather than commonalities. For some, significance comes from providing for the family; for others, from doing meaningful work; some need to make a major contribution to humanity; some require immense wealth. Some people achieve a sense of significance by failure, by being the worst at something, or by having low self-esteem. Whatever the measure of significance, a sense of being important is necessary to all human beings.

Code words for significance are *pride, importance, standards, achievement, performance, perfection, evaluation, discipline, competition,* and *rejection.*

Love/Connection

The fourth need is for the experience of love and connection. Everyone needs connection with other human beings, and everyone strives for and hopes for love. An infant needs to be loved and cared for during a long period of time if it is to develop normally. Infants who are not held and touched will die. This need for love continues throughout our lives. It is epitomized by the concept of romantic love, the one person who will devote their life to us and make us feel complete. In some cultures, romantic love doesn't exist; it's replaced by the love of relatives, friends, and tribe. Some people rarely experience love, but they have many ways of feeling connection with others—in the community or in the workplace. The need to be loved is characteristic of all human beings. Code words for love/connection are *togetherness, passion, unity, warmth, tenderness,* and *desire.*

Growth

The fifth need is for growth. When we stop growing, we die. We need to constantly develop emotionally, intellectually, and spiritually. We grow and change physically as we develop from infancy to adulthood and old age. We grow and change emotionally with every experience, and we grow intellectually as we respond to events and to the world around us. Anything that you want to remain in your life—your money, your health, your relationship, your happiness, love—must be cultivated, developed, expanded. Otherwise, it will degenerate. Some people satisfy the need to grow by working out physically or by reading books. Others need to study and learn constantly in order to feel that they are truly growing.

Contribution

The sixth need is for contribution—to go beyond our own needs and to give to others. A life is incomplete without the sense that one is making a contribution to others or to a cause. It is in the nature of human beings to want to give back, to leave a mark on the world. Giving to others may mean giving time to community service, making a charitable donation, planting trees, writing a book, or giving to one's children. Not only can everyone contribute in some way, but contribution is essential to a sense of fulfillment and to happiness.

The first four needs—certainty, variety, love, and significance—are essential for human survival. They are the fundamental needs of the personality—everyone must feel that they have met them on some level, even if they have to lie to themselves to do so. The last two needs, growth and contribution, are essential to human fulfillment. They are the needs of the spirit, and not everyone finds a way to satisfy them, although they are necessary for lasting fulfillment.

When our needs for love, growth, and contribution are satisfied, they tend to encompass all our other needs. When we focus on something beyond ourselves, most of our problems and sources of pain become less significant. Contribution is the human need that effectively regulates your other five needs. If you are focused on contributing to others, you have the certainty of being able to contribute (there is always a way); you have variety (contribution is highly interactive); you have significance, because you know you are helping others and improving their lives; the spiritual bond created when you help others gives you a deep sense of connection; and you grow by creatively helping others.

For Better or Worse

Everyone experiences the same six human needs. However, everyone finds different ways of satisfying these needs. Each of these needs can be met in ways that are positive or negative. Some ways of satisfying these needs are good for the person, good for others, and good for society, and some are bad for everyone.

The need for certainty can be met by going to school and obtaining a degree that will ensure the possibility of making a good living. Or it can be met by doing as little as possible and avoiding challenges. It can be met by stealing from others and hoarding money and material possessions. Or it can be satisfied by holding rigidly to a dogma or a doctrine.

The need for uncertainty/variety can be met by reading on different subjects and meeting different kinds of people. Or it can be met by engaging in high-risk sports or by risking one's life through violent behavior. It can be met by engaging in extramarital affairs or simply by watching a movie once in a while.

The need for significance can be met by being the best at something—or by being the worst.

The need for love and connection can be satisfied through performing good deeds and being kind, or by dominating others who are forced to show appreciation.

One can grow into becoming a better person—or a despicable human being.

One can contribute to the destruction of others—or to the well-being of many.

As in everything human, there are paradoxes involved in the experience of these needs. A person may have a strong need for certainty, but also a strong need for uncertainty, and therefore might constantly suffer an inner conflict as to which need is most important to satisfy. The need for significance is often contradictory with the need for love. It's difficult to love someone who always has to feel significantly important. That is why so many successful people, who satisfy their need for significance, have trouble in their close relationships and often feel that they are not truly loved.

Let's look at a couple who came to Tony Robbins's workshop and were brave enough to expose the problems in their relationship and to ask Tony to help them. Tony did so by going beyond their apparent problem and connecting them to their deep needs that weren't being fulfilled. Paul and Jenn's story is not unique.

Paul and Jenn

Paul and Jenn were a very nice couple in their mid-thirties, two people who cared for each other deeply. But they were making each other miserable.

After 9 years of a marriage that had produced two little children, Paul had been threatening divorce for 2 years. He talked about leaving Jenn, but he couldn't make up his mind to do it for fear that he would lose his identity and his sense of self-worth. Jenn was overweight when they married and had become more so after the births of their children. Paul didn't feel physically attracted to her, yet he knew that he wanted her love. He admired her for the kind, generous, compassionate person that she was and for her strength and sense of humor.

Jenn lived in fear of Paul's moods and threats and turned to the children for love and companionship. She had stopped working after the birth of the first child, so with only one income the couple had serious financial difficulties. As a result, Jenn had great uncertainty about her marriage and about the family's finances.

Paul and Jenn had talked many times about how he was not attracted to her. But could there be something else other than her physical appearance that kept them apart?

Paul's threats of leaving the marriage gave him power in the relationship because Jenn was afraid of expressing her true feelings for fear that he would leave. The person who threatens abandonment always has the greater power, but it's at the cost of living unhappily. Because of the threats, Jenn could not connect to Paul, and she looked for connection outside of her marriage, with her children, her family, and food.

The person who threatens abandonment not only has greater power but also derives a sense of significance, of being important, from this threat. When a spouse and parent threatens to leave a marriage, that threat becomes the most important issue facing the family. Could it be that Paul felt so insignificant that he had to resort to this threat?

Jenn's family helped them financially. Paul felt diminished because they had to accept this help and he couldn't be the sole source of support. Also, Jenn had great love for her children, her sister, and her family. Paul felt like he came fourth, fifth, or sixth in the order of importance of her loved ones. So a problem that seemed to have only to do with her physical appearance actually went much deeper.

Paul buried himself in work and didn't want to come home because he felt his wife loved everyone else more than she loved him.

Paul was powerful in the relationship because of his threat to leave. But Jenn was powerful because of her family and her money. Each had a source of power that divided them as a couple.

When a couple is in conflict, they typically feel uncertain and insignificant in relation to each other. So they seek to meet these needs outside of the marriage, with the consequence that their relationship is weakened.

Jenn tried to derive certainty from her family and children. And Paul derived significance from the threat of leaving the marriage.

Two Primary Needs

Like Paul and Jenn, most of us focus primarily on two of the six needs. These two prevail over all others and become the primary driving force in our lives. These two needs are experienced so intensely that we will do almost anything to satisfy them. And when these needs are not being fulfilled, any relationship is in grave danger. When you identify a person's two most important needs, you discover that person's driving motivation, what gives meaning and a sense of satisfaction to his or her life. In the workbook section at the end of this book, you will find a series of questions that help you explore your needs.

A person who pursues certainty will make different choices than a person who pursues love. People who share the same primary need can meet that need in very different ways. One person may give herself the feeling of certainty by always controlling her environment and those around her; another person may give himself certainty by not trusting anyone; and a third person may give herself the feeling of certainty by having a deep religious faith.

Jenn's top two needs were for certainty and for love and connection, in that order. For Jenn, fulfilling her need for certainty meant that she had to feel financially secure, which at the time she was not. Since certainty came first and it was not fulfilled, her love could not flow freely. She couldn't allow herself to love unless she felt certainty. Certainty was so important to her that when she felt uncertain, everything in her world disappeared, including her other needs. When certainty is valued over all else, it is difficult to focus on the needs that lead to fulfillment—love, growth, and contribution.[2]

On a scale from 1 to 10, with 10 being absolute certainty, Jenn felt that her certainty with Paul was at a 2, and to feel comfortable she needed at least a 7.

With respect to her children, however, Jenn felt that her certainty was 10. She felt a sense of significance in relation to them at an 8, growth and contribution at a 9. With respect to her family, Jenn felt certainty at 10, love at 10, significance at an 8, and variety at a 7. Jenn felt that her children and her family loved her unconditionally. She didn't feel her husband's love was unconditional.

Paul did not provide Jenn with her number one need for certainty. Jenn did not provide Paul with his top two priorities: the significance and love and connection that come from being valued as a husband. Since they were not meeting their needs through each other, they had to find other ways of meeting them. Jenn got certainty from her kids, her family, her family's money, and food. Paul got significance from being slim (which she was not), from burying himself in work, and from flaunting his threat to leave the marriage.

When both partners are getting their needs met externally, who are they to each other? It is very difficult to sustain love for your spouse when your basic needs are met elsewhere.

The six human needs are the most effective way to track our level of happiness and fulfillment in our relationships. Once we understand how we satisfy our most important needs, we can see clearly what we need to change. It is important to differentiate between needs and vehicles—the actions, beliefs, and behaviors one uses to meet one's needs. Most people have the illusion that vehicles are needs, but they're not. For example, you might think that your primary need is to have money, but money is not a need. It is a vehicle for getting what you really want—which may be love, significance, certainty, or any one of the other three human needs.

Jenn values both love and certainty. But because she values certainty more, she cannot express or feel love until her need for certainty is fulfilled. Her family and her children are the vehicle by which she gets that certainty. If Jenn valued love more than certainty, she could continue to express her love, even when she lacked certainty. When Jenn comes to understand clearly that she is valuing certainty more than love and connection, it becomes possible for her to understand her past decisions and change her priorities to value love and connection above certainty.

In the workbook section, you will learn step-by-step how you can evaluate, understand, and change your priorities. The way we prioritize our needs is not out of our control. If you are unhappy in a significant area of your life, it's time to reflect on what your two most important human needs really are. You might then realize that the way you currently prioritize your needs is not conducive to your well-being or happiness. Like Jenn, you might have certainty at the top of your list, and you might think that because you have a great deal of uncertainty—for instance, financially—certainty has to be at the top. But that is not necessarily the case. Many people live with great uncertainty, and yet they make love and connection their first priority. You can do that, too. You can choose, for example, to put love or contribution at the top of your list, and you can decide to let love flow from you no matter how little certainty there is in your life.

For most people, the need for love and connection supersedes all other needs. Even when it is not acknowledged, the deepest need is for love.

The two primary fears most people have are the fear of not being enough—not being worthy or significant—and the fear of not being loved. Most people need to feel worthy and significant in order to feel loved. Some children grow up feeling that they have to get good grades in order to be loved. Many adults feel that they have to become successful or make money in order to be loved by their families. We can see how this type of fear plays out in Paul's story.

Many of the challenges that arise in our relationships develop because we are constantly trying to satisfy our own basic human needs through other people, while at the same time we are trying to satisfy the basic human needs of those we care for.

The Key to Everlasting Love

In the most fulfilling relationships, all of our six human needs are met through the relationship, be it with spouse, family, friends, or colleagues.

When you satisfy two of the needs of someone else, you have a connection. If you satisfy four of their needs, you have a strong attachment. If you satisfy all six of their human needs, the person is permanently bonded to you.[3]

Naturally, you want to satisfy your partner's needs because it is good for them, good for the relationship, and therefore good for you. If you want a strong, loving, and lasting relationship with your partner, you need to satisfy their six basic human needs.

Understanding and satisfying the human needs of others is the key to a relationship, because it guarantees love and connection. It is equally important that you truly understand your own needs—which two are most motivating you, and which are most motivating your partner? In the workbook section, I will give you a strategy for analyzing this in terms of yourself and your partner, but the same applies to your children, your parents, your friends and colleagues, your boss, and your employees.

Every Individual, Family, and Organization Has a Life Cycle[4]

Our most important needs change over time. Just as there are stages of development from infancy, to childhood, to adolescence, each with its own characteristics and obstacles to overcome, so there are stages in the development of adult life.

Families also have a life cycle that consists of stages:

1. The Courtship Period
2. Early Marriage
3. Childbirth and Dealing with the Young
4. Middle Marriage
5. Weaning Parents from Children
6. Retirement and Old Age

The birth of the first child, when the couple becomes a triad, presents many challenges. The father might feel excluded, the mother may feel abandoned, everyday life changes drastically, and the couple is flooded with new emotions and responsibilities.

Another difficult time is when young adult children leave home. With the children gone, the parents have to focus on their relationship as a couple once more, and sometimes they find that all they had in common was the children. Sometimes a couple may, either deliberately or unconsciously, try to lure one of the children back home, thinking this will preserve the relationship. When a young person feels that his parents' relationship is falling apart because of his absence, he may begin to fail at school or at work, become disturbed or drug addicted, and collapse back home. The parents once again focus on the child. Their relationship once again makes sense, but with terrible consequences for their child.

With the enormous incidence of divorce today, it is possible that divorce has become a stage in the life cycle, and so have remarriage and the formation of a stepfamily. There is not much precedent in the history of the family for these stages, and so they are particularly difficult to navigate.

Problems in a relationship are often an expression of the difficulty in making the transition from one stage of the family life cycle to another. A couple's primary needs change as they go through the life cycle.

During the Courtship Period and Early Marriage, because of the youth of both partners and/or the novelty of the relationship, uncertainty and growth are top priorities—stimulation, entertainment, and learning. As they enter the stage of Childbirth and Dealing with the Young, the couple's needs change. The wife may find that she wants to have more security (certainty) for herself and the children, and she needs to feel the emotional support (love and connection) of the husband. The husband, on the other hand, as the wife gives attention to the children, might feel excluded. His need for reassurance (significance) that he is important as a father and provider may increase. On the other hand, he might have difficulty transitioning to an emphasis on the wife's need for security and emotional support, and he may lose passion for his wife, as she no longer has the same enthusiasm for uncertainty—stimulation, entertainment, and learning. This is the time when the couple, if they want to preserve the marriage, has to be especially alert and careful to satisfy each other's most important needs.

A Tale of Appreciation

Mariah and Chris were both lawyers. They fell in love at law school and were happily married for 2 years, working in the same law firm, until they decided to have children. With the birth of the first child, they decided that Mariah would quit work to be a stay-at-home mom.

At first Chris seemed happy with this decision, but soon he began to comment once in a while about how he envied Mariah for staying at home with their son and how he disliked his work. By the time the second child was born 2 years later, the relationship was stressed almost to the breaking point. Chris worked long hours in hopes of becoming a partner in the law firm. He hated his work and openly expressed his resentment for Mariah because she was at home with the children. He became distant, cold and insisted that he had to have total control of the money since he was the one making it.

Mariah offered to trade places with Chris and go to work so he could stay home with the children. But at this point she could not generate the same level of income that he made, since she had been out of the work world for several years. The couple had financial obligations they had to meet.

Both Mariah and Chris were miserable, but Mariah finally managed to turn the situation around. She realized that she was not meeting Chris's need for significance. In the past, she and Chris had shared many conversations about their work as lawyers. Mariah realized that she had become so focused on the children and so distant from the work world that Chris had lost her as a work buddy and confidant. She understood that this was a real loss for him in their relationship. She also made the effort to understand how difficult and frustrating Chris's work was and how he might have preferred to be in her shoes as a stay-at-home mom.

She began to tell him regularly how much she appreciated the effort and the sacrifice that he made to support the family. She expressed her admiration for Chris at every opportunity and told him how much she loved him. At first Chris was unresponsive, but gradually he warmed up to Mariah again. She set a date for when she would go back to work—when the youngest child was in first grade. She also told Chris that she was happy and appreciative of the way he handled the money. Mariah saved her marriage by focusing on what Chris really needed and making sure that she gave him the recognition that he wanted. It took Chris some time to begin to respond positively, but Mariah was patient with him until they were able to recover the love and companionship that they had shared in the past.

It may seem unfair that in order to change a relationship you need to focus on your partner's needs over and above your own. But this is the most quick and effective way of changing a relationship. As in any endeavor you choose in life, once you've chosen a relationship, in order to make it a happy one, you must focus on giving, not on getting.

It is common for couples to start Early Marriage with an emphasis on growth and contribution as they share their ideals. With the birth of children, the emphasis of one of the spouses may shift to certainty and significance, for instance, causing a rift in the marriage. The same difficulties can arise in the stages of Weaning Parents from Children and adjusting to Retirement and Old Age. These stages are often further complicated by the need to care for elderly parents.

Individuals, families, organizations, nations, and civilizations have a life cycle. What is required to stay alive and in one's prime is the ability to change and synchronize our primary needs over time.

Chapter 3

YOUR MODEL
OF THE WORLD

Each one of us develops a model of the world—an internal program that guides us as to what to expect from others, what to expect from ourselves, how we should live our lives, what we need, what we believe, and what we value. When we understand a person's model of the world, we understand what the person experiences as a reward or a punishment, and we understand what brings them pain.

Our model of the world is composed of six components:

1. Our core beliefs
2. Our key decisions
3. Our life values
4. Our references
5. The habitual questions we ask ourselves
6. The emotional states we repeatedly experience

Let's look at each of these components in depth.

1. The Beliefs That Limit Us

We all have a system of beliefs. What is amazing is that most of us never consciously set this system up. It's been downloaded over the years from parents, teachers, peers, and the general culture. These beliefs direct our decisions about family, work, and community.

To understand your beliefs you have to ask yourself the right questions. Ask the right question, and new insights will be revealed to you. Ask a negative question, and you will get a negative answer. A common negative question is "Are you depressed?" Simply asking the question triggers the depressed state. It's like asking, "Are you thinking of the color blue?" You automatically visualize blue. Questions immediately bring back memories. Questions also change the resources available to us. Focusing on negative feelings and emotions tends to generate more of them.

We are deeply influenced by the metaphors we use to view our lives. Ask yourself, "Life is . . . ?" and you will learn a great deal from your answer. There is a big difference between "Life is a game" and "Life is suffering." To succeed in relationships, you must understand the metaphors that you link to your life as well as the metaphors that your loved ones use to think about their lives.

The Theories We Invent

Alex Bavelas, one of the least acknowledged social psychologists of the sixties at Stanford University, had an uncanny ability to define a problem in such a way that our basic assumptions about human nature were questioned. One thing that particularly interested him was how people develop and sustain a belief system. So he designed an experiment.[1]

He built a machine that produced lights and sounds, and he programmed it at random. Bavelas asked Stanford students to sit at the machine and figure out what was the pattern that determined how lights and sounds would come on. Each student developed a theory—a set of beliefs as to how the machine was programmed. At the end of the experiment, after the student had explained his theory, Bavelas told the student that his theory was wrong and the machine was actually programmed at random. The students invariably responded with disbelief. Not only that, but the more complex the theory that the student had developed, the more intensely he attempted to refute Bavelas and to insist that his theory was correct.

The study demonstrates that there is a basic human need to develop a set of beliefs about why things are the way they are, and once these beliefs are developed, it's very difficult to let them go. So we constantly invent theories about our relationships, and even when we suspect that our theories are wrong, we cannot stop acting as if they were true.

Our relationships can be explained in many different ways. Any explanation may be true, and its opposite may also be true. Yet, whatever our theory, we will probably attempt to hold on to it, no matter what.

In another experiment Bavelas had two people, A and B, sit looking at a screen. A partition separated them so they could not see or speak with one another. Each was told he must learn by trial and error how to tell the difference between slides of healthy cells and sick cells. For each slide, he pushed either a button labeled "Healthy" or one labeled "Sick." After the choice was made, a light illuminated, labeling the choice "Right" or "Wrong." Person A received correct feedback; his "Right" lamp lit when he was right, and his "Wrong" lamp lit when he was wrong. Most "A" subjects learned to distinguish healthy from sick cells about 80 percent of the time.

Person B received a different treatment. His "Right" or "Wrong" lamps lit up based not on his own guesses but on Person A's guesses. He didn't know it, but what he was doing was trying to determine order where none could possibly exist. There was no way that "B" could discover that the answers he got did not correlate with his guesses.

After the test, A and B were asked to discuss what they thought the rules were for determining healthy versus sick cells. A's explanations were simple and concrete; B's were subtle and complex. The amazing thing is that, after this discussion, all Bs and nearly all As believed that B had a better understanding of healthy versus sick cells. A was impressed by B's sophisticated "brilliance" and tended to feel inferior because of the simplicity of his own assumptions. The more complicated B's theory, the more likely it was to convince A. In follow-up tests, the Bs showed almost no improvement, but the As' scores dropped because the As had incorporated some of B's completely baseless ideas.

What Bavelas teaches us is that once a tentative explanation has taken hold of our minds, any information to the contrary may produce not corrections but elaborations of the mistaken explanation.

This can easily happen in a relationship, when one partner begins to ascribe motivations to another which are not true. If we look back at Eva and Jerry from Chapter 1, Eva is convinced that Jerry is demonstrating his disrespect for her every time he fails to pick up his clothes. But in fact, Jerry is simply taking off his clothes. He is not thinking that this act has anything to do with his feelings about Eva. As the problem progresses, Eva's interpretation of Jerry's disrespect becomes more and more elaborate and all-encompassing. It is a short leap to see how this type of thinking is at the basis of pseudoscientific and superstitious thinking that has led through the history of the world to the worst atrocities, such as The Inquisition, ideas of racial superiority, and totalitarian ideologies.

These types of human superstitions can also be found in animal behavior. Paul Watzlawick, in his book *How Real Is Real?*, describes the behavior of the Superstitious Rat:[2] A rat is released into a three-foot-long cage. On the far side is a tray of food. Ten seconds after the rat's release, food is dropped into the tray. If the rat gets to the tray before the food is dropped, it gets no food. It takes the rat only two seconds to run to the tray, but before long, the rat figures out that it only gets food if it gets to the tray ten seconds after it enters the cage. So the rat soon begins to overrule its normal inclinations in order to avoid reaching the tray before ten seconds has elapsed. What the rat does during those extra eight seconds seems to the rat essential to getting food. In other words, the rat soon believes that its delaying actions are what produces the appearance of food. Though the rat's behavior during those extra eight seconds varies from rat to rat—some jump, some twirl left or right, some scamper back and forth—each rat repeats the same behavior time after time. The rat believes that it is that particular behavior that produces the food, a false superstition that has nothing to do with the real cause of the appearance of food.

Recent brain research has confirmed that our brains are wired to force us into forecasting.[3] Two areas of the brain, the nucleus accumbens and the anterior cingulated, specialize in recognizing patterns and choosing between conflicting alternatives. They click into life when any stimulus repeats or alternates. Repetition (this fruit is always edible) and alternation (day always follows night) were the two most basic patterns primitive man had to recognize. Our brains now respond to these simple patterns unconsciously, automatically, and involuntarily. We can't stop searching for patterns any more than we can order our hearts to stop beating. What's more, we pounce on patterns almost instantly. Scott Huettel, a neuroscientist at Duke University, recently found that the anterior cingulated begins to anticipate another repetition after a stimulus occurs only twice in a row.[4] However, if a repeating pattern is broken, neurons suddenly flare in the insula, caudate, and putamen—areas of the inner brain that can generate feelings of fear and anxiety.

Huettel also found that the longer a pattern has previously repeated, the more intensely the brain responds when the pattern is broken. The stock market seems to bear out Huettel's findings. A 2002 study by Irene Kim, a finance scholar at the University of Michigan, shows that the more times in a row a company has topped forecasters' expectations, the further its stock drops when it finally falls below analysts' forecasts.[5] While a shortfall after a run of three good earnings reports trims just 3 percent off the price of the average growth stock, a miss after a string of eight positive quarters cuts off an average of 8 percent.

Wolfram Schultz, a neurophysiologist at the University of Cambridge, studies the workings of dopamine, the brain chemical that gives us a "natural high." He found that dopamine is released after an unexpected reward. The less likely or predictable a reward is, the more active the dopamine neurons become, and the longer they fire. This release of dopamine after an unexpected reward makes humans willing to take risks. This is why people play the lottery, gamble, and keep too much money in too few stocks. The prospect of the euphoric effect of winning big prevents us from focusing on how small the odds of winning big actually are.[6]

Ivan Pavlov, a Russian physiologist, conducted classic experiments with dogs. He would ring a bell whenever his laboratory dogs were to be fed. After a while, the dogs would salivate at the mere sound of the bell, before the food even arrived. Dopamine works in a similar way. Once it becomes associated with a particular cue, the brain releases dopamine on that cue—before the gain occurs.

A team of Harvard researchers led by Hans Breiter found a "striking" similarity between the brains of people trying to predict financial rewards and the brains of cocaine addicts and morphine users. Back in the booming bull market of 1999, day traders got a "high" just from sitting down in front of their computers if their previous trades had been profitable. Even more interestingly, if a predicted reward fails to arrive, dopamine in the brain switches off instantly, creating an instant swing from euphoria to depression. This may help to explain why the market overreacts so strongly to any short-term disappointment.[7]

What can we learn from these studies? To begin with, consider that you might need to question the methods by which you arrive at decisions. We have pseudoscientific and superstitious minds, much like the college students who could not stop creating theories and refused to believe that their theories were wrong, or like the rat that believes that it is the somersaults that bring out the food. The theories we invent about ourselves and about others result in decisions that guide our lives.

It is typical for people to believe that their unwanted or undesirable behavior is involuntary. They create a theory about how "they can't help it." The behavior is like a chronic illness, out of their control, and there is nothing they can do about it. Obsessive thoughts, fears, compulsions, addictions, bad temper, all fall into the category of behaviors that are theorized to be involuntary. For example, headaches are often considered involuntary, while stealing cars is considered deliberate, voluntary behavior. Of course, there are exceptions; husbands have been known to believe that their wives deliberately bring on a headache to avoid their sexual overtures, and certain parents of delinquents have gone so far as to propose that there must be a specific brain damage associated with stealing motorcycles.

Usually, the first step in changing unwanted behavior is to believe that the behavior is voluntary and can therefore be changed. This is hard to believe when a person has suffered from undesirable behavior for a long time. But you can create a context to prove to yourself that the behavior is actually voluntary and that you can change it. Let's look at how one woman did just that.

A Trick for Liking Yourself More

Caroline was a beautiful, successful businesswoman from an upper-class family. She was cultured, elegant, and tough. She was married to a man who refused to work and who abused her emotionally and physically. He refused to have sex with her and often insulted her, spat on her face, and dragged her by her hair. This was her second marriage, and she had no children. I suggested divorce. She said she couldn't do that because she was afraid of him and because she had low self-esteem. She felt she deserved this husband. It was almost as if she had a voice inside her head that told her she was stupid, ugly, fat, unfeeling, and unworthy. Her grandmother, whom she had loved very much, had committed suicide, and Caroline thought that she might very well end up doing the same because she had so much self-hatred. She had spent years in therapy, but she couldn't control her self-deprecation. It seemed completely involuntary.

I spent hours arguing that she was beautiful, intelligent, successful, and kind, but to no avail. She said she could see that intellectually, but emotionally she felt she was worthless—it was totally out of her control.

One day I said to her that I was really tired of listening to her self-hatred. If she was going to continue experiencing these thoughts, at least some good should come out of it. I told her that the next time she had a low self-esteem thought, she would immediately write a check for $100, made out to a women's shelter that was in my neighborhood, and mail it. The second time she had a self-deprecating thought, the check would be for $200. The third time it would be for $400, and so on in geometric progression. She never mentioned another low-self-esteem idea to me, and I helped her to divorce her husband, to proceed with her brilliant career, and to marry a very good man.

Months later, I discovered that she had given the shelter several thousand dollars before she found that she could totally control her negative thinking. Once she abandoned her theory that her thoughts were uncontrollable, she could take charge and succeed in other areas of her life. Through the device of writing checks, she was forced to realize that she could actually exert control over her thoughts.

Caroline changed her focus from her habitual feelings of low self-worth to what that habit was costing her—she was able to overcome her habit and contributed to society at the same time!

2. The Key Decisions We Make

Sometimes people make decisions early in childhood to repress and block certain areas of their personality and to focus on developing others. What may work in order to survive in childhood often becomes obsolete in adult life and interferes with every relationship. A man might decide as a boy that boys don't cry, and in blocking his tears might block all his vulnerability and sensitivity. When it's time to be sensitive to his wife and his children, he may not be able to do it. A little girl may stand up to her abusive father and refuse to acknowledge that she's hurt. As a woman, she may be a strong, caring mother, but she may not be able to be vulnerable and loving in a sexual, erotic way with her husband. Often, decisions that are made early in childhood persist into adulthood, long after they have become obsolete, and interfere with our relationships and our happiness.

Key decisions made in early life may have positive consequences, such as the decision to be brave, to persist, or to accomplish. Yet sometimes even the most positive key decisions may result in rejecting important parts of our identity. Sometimes the key decision has only negative consequences and persists through adult life even though it has no apparent value.

We make decisions every moment of every day, but not all decisions are equal. Some run deep and penetrate every aspect of our lives. Other decisions are superficial. We make them and change them quickly and without any major disruption in our lives. We call some extraordinarily powerful decisions "key decisions" because they command and direct other decisions you make in your life. Key decisions are the keys to certain doors of experience. There are many things in life that you simply can't experience unless you've made the key decision that will open that door for you.

There are four qualities that make a decision powerful.

The earlier the decision, the more powerful it will be. We make key decisions every day, but the choices we make today build and depend upon the choices we made yesterday or years ago. For instance, if I decide to drive somewhere today, that decision references a past key decision I made to learn how to drive. The key decision to learn to drive was powerful because it affected an entire area of my life. Now, I am able to drive wherever I choose, and that leads to other opportunities. Other key decisions may be influencing even broader parts of your life, for instance: the decision whether or not to live your life as one of goodness; whether or not to trust people (and whom to trust); whether or not to work hard and what sort of work to focus on. We all have made profound decisions in our past, and these decisions color every aspect of our lives today. The further back we made these decisions, the more profound and influential they are in our lives. Does this mean that it's too late to make new powerful decisions? Of course not. However, we need to go back to the moment we made that decision, to remember why we made it then, and to consciously make a new decision that serves us today.

The more urgent the circumstances, the more influential the decision. Key decisions are usually made in times of emotional intensity and urgency—circumstances push us out of the comfort zone created by previous decisions and throw us into new territory. The most extreme key decisions are made when we are most vulnerable, such as early childhood or in times of illness or war. Sometimes urgency is created by becoming aware of the potential consequences of continuing to live life as you've been living it. Look back to crisis moments in your life, to times of vulnerability, and it is there where you will find your key decisions.

Key decisions set a precedent. Since key decisions take place under pressing situations, they set a precedent for how you will respond to similar situations down the road. Important decisions are usually made when you are truly confused about what to do. You come to a split in the road and don't know how to proceed—the future is hard to predict—you have to choose where to go without knowing where the roads will eventually lead and what lies along them. It is precisely in these times that you have to rise above your own confusion and uncertainty and recognize the necessity of taking action. When you do, you create a new precedent for the future. When you learn to make these decisions more consciously, you give yourself a strong base on which to build the rest of your life.

Key decisions are reinforced with repetition and reward. A decision gains strength when it is reinforced, which leads us to make it again and again. Meeting at least two of our six human needs gives us that reward. If we meet at least two of these needs—certainty, uncertainty, significance, connection, growth, and contribution—we are motivated to make the same decision over and over again. However, the issue is how to meet the six universal needs in ways that are good for yourself and for others.

///////////////////////////

Here's an example of a key decision made at an early age that no longer serves any function in the person's life.

Giving Up an Old Identity

A little Korean orphan girl, Kim, was adopted by an American couple and came to live in the United States. The parents had trouble understanding and bonding with her. Over the years they consulted several therapists. One of the behaviors that they found most disturbing was that Kim would take food from the kitchen and hide it in her room, even though she was not deprived of anything. As she grew older, the parents consulted with me. Kim was still overeating, hoarding food, and sometimes "stealing" small inexpensive objects. What the parents called "stealing" would probably have been simply borrowing in the eyes of another family.

The parents were not a good match for Kim, who was a free spirit, intelligent, and creative, while they were rigid and narrow-minded. I struggled to help them understand that Kim's behaviors of hoarding food, overeating whenever possible, and even stealing had been appropriate for survival when she was a young child, probably living in the streets of Korea. It would take some time for Kim to totally give up her identity as a street urchin and a little thief.

Kim's behavior improved but the parents discontinued the therapy. They had never been happy with my emphasis on tolerance and compassion. Years later I got a phone call from Kim. "Something weird has happened to me," she said, "and I need to talk with you as soon as possible." She was now an attractive young woman in her early twenties. She explained that she had been alienated from her parents for a while but reconciled with them when she had a child out of wedlock. She loved her 3-year-old son and was going to college, working, and quite happy with her life.

What had prompted her call was that one day, out of the blue, she had done something so inappropriate that she was scared and confused. She was looking at some winter jackets in a department store with her son in a stroller when she picked up a jacket and walked out of the store with it, even though she had plenty of money to pay for the jacket. She was arrested and detained for a few hours and was now banned from entering that shopping mall.

She couldn't understand why she had done this, why would she put her son through such an ordeal? Was she crazy? Would she do this again? I reminded her of how as a little girl she had hoarded food and stolen small objects. Kim couldn't remember anything about her life in Korea, but she agreed that she probably had survived in the streets by stealing, perhaps not just for herself but also for her parents.

To have to steal in order to survive must have been extremely frightening for a young child, and she probably had to muster all her strength to be able to do it. With all her energy she must have made the key decision: I am a thief. And it had stayed with her and surfaced from time to time. It was now time to let it go. She was now a mother, a college student, and an administrator, not a thief. She didn't need to steal to survive. She was not crazy. She just had to be watchful and not allow her old identity to creep back into her life. Kim understood and went on to lead a happy and productive life.

3. The Values That Guide Us

What you value determines who you are and who you can become. A person who values security will have a very different life from someone who values adventure. Someone who values caring for others is quite different from someone who values certainty and financial success. When someone who values security marries someone who values adventure, there are possibilities for conflict.

Sometimes a conflict of values lies within the individual. Anthony Robbins developed an interesting method for understanding the values of an individual and the difficulties that might arise from those values.

Robbins asked John, a 45-year-old independent contractor and father of two, to make a list of everything he valued, quickly and spontaneously as it came to mind—as many values as he could think of in a few minutes. Then he asked John to pick the first 10 values on his list and rank them in order of importance, from the most important to the least.

John's list looked like this: adventure, fun, love, contribution, lifestyle, financial security, integrity, trust, harmony, health.

Let's look at John's age and situation in life. Should adventure and fun be at the top of his list? John has a family, yet his family is not on his list. What does that tell us about John? Having love as third after adventure and fun could give us a clue to the nature of his marriage. John's wife might feel that she is not number one in his life. When a spouse feels that they are not number one, trouble is brewing.

It is important that we look at our values through the prism of our age. John is middle-aged, has people who depend on him financially, and a job that is physically demanding. Shouldn't health be higher on his list?

In the workbook section you'll find an exercise to explore your values and those of your partner. It's a good practice to review your values each year, and consciously change them to reflect your current situation and what you truly want now.

This method of analyzing values can be used for different purposes and with different relationships. It's a great method for improving satisfaction at work. I've used it with professional psychotherapists, asking them to list what they value most about being a therapist and then having them specify three ways to fulfill that value each day. The results are powerful. The therapists who felt that they had to be appreciated by every single client on any given day were stressed and miserable. Those who only needed to feel that they had been understanding or that they had tried their best were more likely to be relaxed and happy.

Here's another example: In a comparison between Caucasian and Latino teenagers, the Caucasian teenagers listed friends as their highest value. The Latinos rated family at the top of the list, and friends came second. Family was way down on the list (if present at all) for the Caucasian teens. Guess which group experienced more family conflicts? Guess which kids were more vulnerable to peer pressure?[8]

A Conflict of Values

A family in serious crisis flew halfway around the world to meet with me. The patriarch of the family had built an extraordinarily successful company and had accrued immense wealth. He and his wife had four grown children—two men and two women—and several grandchildren. For many years he had involved his older son in the company, handing him opportunities and responsibilities, but the son had failed at everything he did. Nevertheless, he had been compensated with millions of dollars, a beautiful home, and a great lifestyle. As the father grew older, his health deteriorated, and he had quadruple heart bypass surgery. He decided he needed to work less, so he included the second son and a son-in-law in the business. He told the older son he would no longer be needed, although he would keep his salary and his shares in the company. The son was outraged and demanded $20 million and suggested he would blackmail his own father, making threats about leaking secret information to business competitors or preventing his parents from seeing their grandchildren. The father was outraged. He came to see me with his wife, his older son, and his daughter-in-law.

I met them briefly on the evening they arrived and immediately decided I would not see the four of them together again until I had a solution. The tension was so thick that direct communication would not be productive. When I met with the son and his wife alone, they confirmed their demands clearly and unequivocally. When I conveyed this information to the father, he became angry. His face was flushed, and I could see the veins protruding on his neck. I noticed the concern on his wife's face as she watched her husband become upset. He said, "This is blackmail, this is an injustice. I will never give in."

I listened to him patiently until I was sure that he knew I understood him, and then I said, "This is not about justice. This is about health—your health. If this problem persists, you will die. As you were talking, I could see your blood pressure go up. You've already had bypass surgery. You can't afford to be upset. Give him what he wants for the sake of your health so you and your wife can have the good life you deserve and the grandchildren you love. I know your wife loves you and values your health above all. Let your other son and your son-in-law run the business without conflicts and you can be on vacation."

The wife's face lit up with appreciation. "She's right," she said. "It's the price of our health and our life." The decision was made. By helping the father to change his highest value from justice to health, everything changed.

The son's highest values were his birthright and his status. He had nothing to lose by sticking to his position and threatening the family. The father, however, had a lot to lose: his health, his relationship with his grandchildren, and the well-being of his wife.

4. References

From an early age we learn to imitate and model ourselves on people we love or admire. These people are the references that we use to judge whether or not we are leading the life we want to live and whether we are good enough or have accomplished enough. These references sometimes remain the same throughout our lives and sometimes change as we develop. Sometimes the reference is a person in the older generation—sometimes it is a peer. Through the ages we have known about the importance of having a mentor, a guide, or a teacher in order to succeed in a career or in a spiritual path. The same applies to relationships. If you want to have happy, successful relationships, model yourself on those who do. Whenever possible, surround yourself with friends who have good relationships and look up to those in the older generation who have accomplished what you want to accomplish.

5. Habitual Questions We Ask Ourselves

We constantly ask ourselves questions and, for most of us, two or three questions repeat over and over in our heads. The quality of your relationships depends to a great extent on the quality of the questions you ask yourself. You will have a very different relationship, for example, if you ask yourself, "Why doesn't she/he love me?" rather than asking yourself, "How can I show him/her that I love them in the way they want to be loved?" Similarly, your relationships will be totally different if, instead of asking yourself,

"How can I get him/her to respect me?" you ask yourself, "How can I show respect toward him/her?" When you find that you're asking yourself the same old question and not finding the answer, switch the focus of question so it becomes about what you can do, what is in your control, instead of a question about how to change the other person. When you do this, you are in control and you are empowered.

6. The Emotions That Rule

As hundreds of research studies show, there is no question about the curative power of love and other positive emotions, as well as about the illness-inducing power of negative emotions such as fear and anger. Our emotions are the driving force for all our accomplishments. Human beings are capable of incredible acts of courage because of love, fear, passion, or desire. The wish to feel loved and appreciated can lead to extraordinary accomplishments and to great self-sacrifice. Yet, even though people may recognize the importance of emotions, it's common for them to feel that they have no control over their own emotions.

Many people, who are otherwise successful, fail to control their emotions when their loved ones are involved. A man might handle millions of dollars and hundreds of employees on a daily basis, yet he might come home and a simple question from his wife may trigger a fit of rage more appropriate to a 5-year-old than a grown-up in his position in the world. Just the common phrase "She (or he) made me angry" is a curious expression. How can someone else make you feel an emotion that you don't want to experience? Emotions are in your heart, in your mind, they are part of you, not part of somebody else.

Not only do most people doubt that they can control their emotions, but they actually experience emotions that are obsolete. Fear and anxiety, for example, may have been appropriate emotions at the time someone was facing a dangerous situation. Yet fear and anxiety can continue over time even when there is no imminent danger. Research suggests that emotions serve as a central organizing process within the brain. Our emotions directly shape our experiences and help us to adapt to future stressors. Emotions control and regulate how we process information and what we do about it. That is, emotions are a higher function of the brain that organizes us as to what to pay attention to, what it means, and what to do about it.

There is a series of steps by which emotions regulate our thinking and our behavior.[9]

First, something happens, an event we focus on. In most circumstances we can choose what we focus on. For example, I am told that there was violence in my children's school but that my children are safe. I could focus on how angry I am that there would be violence and worry that my children will never be safe at school again, or I can focus on how to prevent further violence, among many other possibilities. Once we have focused on something, we immediately assign it an emotional meaning: Is this good or bad? Almost simultaneously our physiology changes according to whether the meaning is positive or negative. Then we choose what emotional reaction we will have. Will it be sadness, anger, fear, joy (since my children are safe), shame, disgust, or surprise? Then we decide what action to take depending on the emotion that prevails. If it is sadness, we might cry; if it's anger, we might fight; fear will make us hide or run away, and so on. The same event can trigger a different focus, meaning, physiology, emotion, and therefore action in different people.

Most people don't experience a broad range of emotions in their lives. They are limited to only a few that they experience over and over again. So, no matter what the events, they will experience the same emotion that they regularly experience in their lives. Let's say there is a natural disaster or a robbery. The person who is frequently sad will feel sad; the angry person will be angry; the fearful one will be afraid; and so on. We operate our patterns of emotion that give meaning to events and determine what we do and the meaning we give to life. These patterns are usually established early on in life, and by the time we become adults they are obsolete. But they continue to dominate our behavior, like bad habits, even though frequently they don't lead to the outcomes we would prefer.

On September 11, 2001, Tony Robbins was teaching a seminar in Hawaii to more than 2,000 people. He asked them to express what emotion they experienced on hearing the tragic news of the terrorist attack. Some people felt sad; others were enraged; some felt guilty for not being in New York to help; some were indifferent; and some were frightened. These emotions were the same ones that these individuals typically experienced on a regular basis. The terrorist attacks didn't bring out new emotions. The sad person felt sad; the angry person was enraged; the guilty one felt guilty; the indifferent one didn't care; and the fearful one was frightened.

Emotions pervade all mental functions and create meaning in life. Emotion and meaning are created by the same processes. Thought and emotion are by nature inseparable. It follows logically that we can control our emotions by having the thoughts that we want to experience.[10]

Words have tremendous power to influence emotions. By changing your vocabulary, especially the words that you consistently use to describe emotions, you can change how you think, feel, and interact with others. For example, if instead of saying you are angry or enraged when you are upset at someone, you force yourself to minimize the intensity of what you're feeling and say, "I'm feeling a tad out of sorts" or "I'm a bit peeved." Wouldn't this irony make you smile? Wouldn't it change the nature of the interaction? If instead of thinking, "I'm depressed," you said to yourself, "I'm bored" or "I'm tired," wouldn't this change your focus?

Here's how one woman was able to consciously exert control over her emotions and, ultimately, change them.

Ex-Obsession

Ruth came to see me because she was very worried about obsessive thoughts of hatred for her ex-husband. She had always been a good-natured person but was caught in a bad marriage. Eventually, she and her husband divorced, and soon he was remarried to a much younger woman. He was in a good financial position, while Ruth was struggling with work she didn't particularly enjoy. She found that increasingly she was having intrusive thoughts about hating her husband, wishing him illness and death, and was filled with anger and resentment. She was tearful when she explained to me that she didn't like the person that she was becoming, but she couldn't stop having those thoughts. They were completely involuntary. I was sympathetic to her plight but explained that there were alternatives to experiencing these negative thoughts. Every morning she would get up 20 minutes earlier than usual, and she would sit in a special chair that she placed in her bedroom just for this purpose. For 20 minutes she would concentrate on having bad thoughts about her husband: how mean he was, how she hated him, how she wished him dead, and so forth. I explained that the mind tends to wander, so she would find it difficult to avoid having other kinds of thoughts, but it was important to keep forcing her mind back to the hateful thoughts about her husband. In 20 minutes she would stop and get on with her day. If during the day any hateful thoughts about her husband came to her mind, she would say to herself, "I'm not going to think about that now. I have 20 minutes to think about that tomorrow morning," and she would force her mind away from the hateful thoughts.

When she saw me again 2 weeks later, she reported that she had faithfully done the exercise and she no longer had hateful thoughts during the day, but in those 20 minutes early in the morning she had found that her mind wandered toward hateful thoughts about me! We laughed as she asked me for how much longer would she have to do this exercise. I didn't want to let her off too easily, so I insisted that she should continue for a few weeks, but soon Ruth decided the exercise was no longer necessary. She wasn't thinking about the ex-husband at all and was focused on improving at work and making new friends.

Our Model of the World: For Good or Ill

Our model of the world can either lead us to a fulfilling life, or set us up for continuous disappointment. Let's look at two examples.

John is a businessman whose most important needs are certainty and significance. To meet those needs, he feels he needs to make a million dollars each year (he is currently making half a million) and be respected by everyone he knows, even his teenage children. His highest values are success and pride (which means he has to be successful and proud in every area of his life: business, family, community, even his weight—he is now 30 pounds overweight). His preferred emotions are being admired and being appreciated, and this has to be expressed by everyone he meets on any given day. Has John set himself up to feel miserable most of the time? What are the chances that his teenage children will appreciate and respect him? Or that he will lose the 30 pounds? Or make a million dollars every year?

For Bill, in contrast, the most important needs are love and growth. To meet those needs, he has to hug his children and read a book. His highest values are gratitude and compassion. To meet these values, he has to think about how grateful he is for his health and his family's well-being, and he has to do some charitable work. His preferred emotions are joy and enthusiasm. To meet them, he has to take a walk in nature and do something interesting at work.

Clearly Bill has set himself up for a happier life than what John can expect.

It is in your power to choose the values, needs, and emotions that you want to experience.

Chapter 4

TRIANGLES, CIRCLES, AND WHO'S ON TOP?

Everything in the world consists of repeating shapes and patterns. There are two basic shapes in our world: the triangle and the circle. All other shapes derive from these two. The sphere, the grape, the human head, the hand, the atom, the spider's web, the organization of government, the web of science and technology, the family, and the relationships we form during the course of our lives—all form triangles or circles.[1]

Every human organization consists of variations and combinations of these two basic shapes. One might think that dyads exist—relationships between just two people—but the dyad tends to immediately become a triangle. When two people get together and define a relationship, immediately a third person interferes, and the relationship becomes a triangle.

Two people get married—they form a dyad; a child is born—now they are a triangle. A man and a woman fall in love—they are a dyad; her father interferes—they have become a triangle. Two men are partners at work—they form a dyad; their wives dislike each other—the relationship between the partners becomes triangulated with their wives.

A circle is a group of friends, a team, a band. Circles are relationships between equals involving more than three people. All organizations are combinations of triangles and circles.

The concept of the triangle is the basis of all drama. Greek tragedy and Shakespearean drama centered on conflicted triangles. The triangle is also at the foundation of psychology: the mother, the father, and the child, from which the idea of the Oedipus conflict derives. The Holy Trinity is the foundation of Christianity.

In triangles there is hierarchy, with one or two people in a superior position to the others. Circles are egalitarian. A circle can transform into a series of triangles, however, when it takes the form of a wheel with a leader in the center who has authority over everyone in the circle.[2]

Which form of organization is more efficient: the triangle or the circle? Alex Bavelas designed experiments to test three different types of organizational models: the Wheel, which resembles the typical organizational structure; the Chain, a slight modification of the Wheel; and the Circle, where everyone communicates in a network of equality.

The results of the experiments showed that the Wheel, the form most like the top-down leadership model, was the most accurate and the most efficient for simple tasks. Even though the central person reported high morale, the other members did not enjoy the experiment. When the tasks were more complex, the Circle was the more efficient and accurate, and all members claimed relatively high morale. The connection to our current work environments is obvious. Warren Bennis has been known to say, "None of us is as smart as all of us." That is, all of us together are smarter than any one of us individually.

Triangles usually divide into a coalition of two members against a third. The most distinctive characteristics of triadic systems are that strength can result in weakness and weakness can be transformed into strength. Sociologist Theodore Caplow, PhD, has provided the most extensive analysis of coalitions in triads, and he points out an interesting possibility.[3]

Suppose there are three thieves—Tom, Dick, and Harry—who live isolated from authority. Dick and Harry are equal in strength, but Tom is slightly stronger. Tom could overpower Dick and Harry individually, but he could be easily overpowered by Dick and Harry together. If Tom tries to form a coalition with Dick or Harry, neither Dick nor Harry has a reason to want to be in that coalition since Tom would be a partner who threatens to dominate, whereas in a coalition between Dick and Harry, there would be no threat of domination since both are equal. It is clear that Tom's margin of superiority ensures his defeat. If Tom can divest himself of his superiority, becoming equal to Dick and Harry, his chances of joining a winning coalition would then be 2 to 1, since all coalitions are equally likely in egalitarian triads. What's even more surprising is that if Tom could become considerably weaker than both Dick and Harry, he would be sought out by both as a coalition partner, and he could make his own terms with any one of the two. The transformation of strength to weakness and of weakness to strength in the triad helps to explain the balance struck between the rulers and the ruled in every human society.

Triangles also exhibit certain catalytic effects. The presence of an antagonist increases our affection for a friend, and the presence of a friend increases one's hostility toward a common antagonist. It is interesting to notice how quickly a bond is created between people who have a common hatred for a political leader, even though they may have nothing else in common. Another catalytic effect has to do with organizations. Much of the world's work is accomplished by hierarchical triads such as leader-lieutenant-follower, master-journeyman-apprentice, or manager-foreman-worker. Each of these has a man in the middle bearing the brunt of the tension between discipline and freedom by sustaining nearly incompatible relationships with his superior and his subordinate.

Most institutions in today's world are organized in triangles with rigid hierarchies, and most people live in families that are organized as triangles. Perhaps that is why there seems to be a general longing to belong to circles, to communities, to groups of friends. But to have a balanced life, it is necessary to belong to both triangles and circles.

The Power of Peers

Marion had two adult daughters to whom she was very close. The daughters frequently ganged together against their mother, criticizing, blaming, and attacking her. Eventually, Marion decided she needed stronger peer relationships to counter the power that her daughters had over her. She became active in a local charity that took up most of her time. There, she developed many friends. She no longer had time to listen to the daughters or to interact with them. Even though she continued to be available to them, her circle of friends and co-workers was more important. Having less contact with the daughters, she was able to have less conflict with them.

Let's look again at Paul and Jenn's situation. Paul's father died when Paul was very young. He was raised by a mother and four older sisters who adored him. This was his circle from which he received unconditional love. The mother and the sisters, however, rejected Jenn, feeling that Paul could have done better. Paul's mother was a devout Catholic, and Jenn was not Catholic. Paul was caught in a conflicting triangle between his wife and the five women in his family.

Jenn's father had died recently. Jenn had been his favorite child, and he had told her that she was "perfect." He had been successful, strong, and very giving to Jenn. While her father was alive, Jenn was caught in a triangle between Paul and her father. Jenn's best friend was her sister, in whom she confided and to whom she turned when she was upset. Here was another triangle where Jenn often seemed to appreciate her sister more than she appreciated her husband. Jenn's love for her children was unconditional, and she knew that she could satisfy all her needs through them. This closeness to her children resulted in a distance from her husband. In addition, Jenn's mother helped her financially, creating yet another triangle where once again Paul was excluded.

Cross-Generational Coalitions

In most organizations, families, and relationships there is hierarchy: One person has more power and responsibility than another. In hierarchical organizations and relationships, there is a tacit or explicit contract for the way power and benefits are distributed. The person who provides benefits that are necessary for the survival and well-being of others—for example, the breadwinner of a family or in the case of Jenn and Paul, Jenn because she gets money from her family—is more powerful than those who are dependent on him or her.

In a family, parents are in a position superior to that of their children: Parents have legal responsibility to provide for and take care of their children. The hierarchical organization of a family includes some members dominating, taking responsibility, and making decisions for others. It also includes helping, protecting, comforting, reforming, and taking care of others.

The benefits parents derive from their children's love and concern are of a different order and magnitude from those they provide by ensuring the children's physical survival and well-being. Indeed, the family unit originated in order to care for the young.

Throughout history, hierarchical differences between the generations have been clear. It can be argued that the helpless baby who cries for attention has more power over the mother than the mother has over the baby—and it certainly has more power than do the older siblings. Undoubtedly, a baby can derive power over the family from crying, but this power is insignificant compared to the family's power to neglect, harm, or lovingly care for the baby. The benefits parents and children obtain from their relationships are repeatedly renegotiated as children grow older and the family constellation varies.

In a marriage, the spouses usually balance the hierarchy by dividing spheres of power and responsibility. A husband might make all the financial decisions, while his wife makes all the decisions involving relatives. Or a husband might predominate in decisions involving children, while his wife takes charge of friends and extended family. In these ways, a couple has several hierarchical relationships; one of the spouses is superior in certain areas but inferior in others.

Just as power can be malign or benign, a hierarchy can be undesirable or benevolent. It all depends on a person's point of view.

Once, in a group of student therapists, a Baptist minister commented on the advantages of his religion, saying, "No one is above me to tell me what to do." Later, in private, one of the teachers, a Catholic, reflected, "These Baptist ministers are so alone; no one is above them to help them." The Baptist and the Catholic had different views of the function of a superior.

Whenever there is hierarchy, there is the possibility of cross-generational coalitions. A husband and wife may argue over the way the wife spends money. At a certain point in time, the wife might enlist the older son in a coalition against the husband. Mother and son may talk disparagingly about the father and to the father and secretly plot about how to influence or deceive him. The wife's coalition with the son gives her power in relation to the husband and limits the husband's power over how the wife spends money. The wife now has an ally in her battle with her husband, and the husband now runs the risk of alienating his son. Such a cross-generational coalition can stabilize a marriage, but it creates a triangle that weakens the position of both husband and wife. Now the son has a source of power over both of them.

Cross-generational coalitions take different forms in different families. A grandparent may side with a grandchild against a parent. An aunt might side with a niece against her mother. A husband might join his mother against his wife. These alliances are most often covert and are rarely expressed in verbal conversation. They involve painful conflicts that can continue for years.

A Mother and Child Coalition

Susan wished to stay at home and raise her children. Her husband, Mike, wanted her to go back to work and bring in a second income. Susan and Mike argued and struggled about this problem, often in the presence of their son, Joey. Joey had some learning difficulties that seemed to be manageable with some special help from the school. Susan believed that she should be a stay-at-home mom to help Joey with his homework. Mike thought this was unnecessary. Finally, Susan gave in and began to look for work. At that point Joey refused to go to school. Every morning was a struggle—he wouldn't get up, he felt sick, he didn't like the school. Now Joey had a serious problem, and Susan had a reason to stop looking for work and stay at home. She had to struggle every morning with Joey and help him to overcome his school problems. The issue of Susan going to work was no longer an issue between Susan and Mike. Joey, consciously or unconsciously, had made a tacit, or unspoken, coalition with his mother. He might have even contributed to saving the parents' marriage, but at the cost of his own health and well-being.

Sometimes cross-generational coalitions are overt. A wife might confide her marital problems to her child and in this way antagonize the child against the father. Parents may criticize a grandparent and create a conflict in a child who loves both his grandparent and his parents. Such a situation can cause a child to feel conflicted and cause him great suffering because his loyalties are divided.

Every cross-generational coalition involves a conflict of loyalty. These coalitions, as well as the conflicts they engender, are often disguised and not easily discovered. Let's look at a husband who is closer to his mother than to his wife. When he complains about his wife to his mother, he is being disloyal to his wife. The wife becomes more and more disempowered, and begins to suffer from "depression," without realizing that the source of her depression is her husband's relationship to his mother.

Cross-generational coalitions become extremely complex in family-owned businesses, causing tremendous stress. For example, when a husband and wife are running a business, the husband might be in a coalition with his mother in the realm of family life, and with an employee in the realm of the business. The wife is excluded and secondary both at home and at work. Sometimes the business is used to compensate and balance for cross-generational coalitions in the family: The husband is in a coalition with his mother, so the wife forms a coalition with an employee at work. Or the wife is in a coalition with an employee, against her husband, so her husband develops a coalition with their child against the wife.

Cross-generational coalitions are not always the result of an antagonistic relationship. A father may be intensely involved with his son, excluding the mother from the relationship—not intentionally but simply because he enjoys being close to his son. The child, however, may suffer from the distance or estrangement from the mother. Jennifer's story, below, illustrates this point.

Connecting a Father to His Son

Jennifer was an energetic, creative entrepreneur. She started her own marketing company, and eventually her husband, Joe, quit his job and came to work for her. They had two little boys. One of them, Jimmy, was very attached to Jennifer and didn't get along so well with his father. Jennifer often had to travel for the company, and Joe stayed home with the children. Even when Jennifer wasn't traveling, she often worked longer hours than Joe. On those occasions, either Joe or Jimmy constantly called her on her cell phone asking for permission to do something, giving her information on what they were supposed to do, or requesting that she mediate in a quarrel between them.

After listening to a lecture I gave on cross-generational coalitions, Jennifer decided to take action. On her next trip out of town she turned off her cell phone. For 3 days Joe and Jimmy could not communicate with her. They had to work out their problems without Jennifer's input. When she came back, Joe said to her, "I know what you were doing—don't ever do that to me again. But it worked. Jimmy and I now get along famously." And they did; Jimmy never had a problem connecting to his father again. By staying out of the relationship between Joe and Jimmy, Jennifer had allowed them to develop a relationship of their own.

Every Hierarchy Contains the Possibility of Incongruity

When John became an adolescent, he started acting out, breaking curfew, coming home obviously inebriated. His parents were very concerned about him and tried various interventions to change his behavior. Suddenly, John had power over his parents, who were focused on helping him but were ineffective. It was John's behavior that began to determine what the family could and could not do, what they talked about, how they spent their time, and so on. But because John was clearly disturbed and in trouble, his parents had to take care of him and focus on him more than they had since he was a young child.

So this family was in two conflicting hierarchical arrangements. Both John and his parents were simultaneously in a superior and an inferior position in relation to each other. As the situation escalated, and John's parents were not able to turn around his behavior, they found themselves in a hierarchical reversal. The parents lost all the power to John, who dominated them by terrorizing them with worry over his behavior.

Likewise, if a husband develops problem behavior—say, alcoholism—two incongruous hierarchies are simultaneously defined in the marriage. The alcoholic husband is in an inferior position because of his addictive and destructive behavior, while his wife is put in the superior position of helper. Yet, at the same time, the husband is in a superior position if he refuses to be influenced and helped, while the wife is put in the inferior position. Her life becomes organized around her husband's needs and problems.

Symmetrical Relations and Power Struggles

Symmetrical relations are those in which all parties vie for equal power in the same areas of control and expertise. For example, usually the relationship between students in a classroom is symmetrical, while the relationship between the students and the teacher is complementary. Complementary relationships are those in which the parties have unequal power, control, and expertise. In the extreme, one person orders and the others obey. Most institutions in our culture—corporations, universities, the government, and the military—are organized on a model of complementary relationships.

The most stable couples are those that have complementary relationships. A traditional complementary relationship, over many centuries, has been one where the husband works, brings home a paycheck, and hands it over to his wife. She manages the home and the children and pays the bills, deciding how money will be spent. In this way, each spouse has different areas of responsibility, and each has power over different aspects of life. He has power as a breadwinner and provider; she has power over spending and family relationships. Each depends on the other, and so the relationship will tend to be stable. The fact that a relationship is stable, however, doesn't mean that it's satisfactory. For a relationship to be happy, there has to be a mix of symmetry and complementarity. In a traditional marriage, like the one above, there may be areas of the couple's life in which they are equal and symmetrical, such as their passionate sex life, their contribution to a cause, or their love of music.[4]

Truly complementary marriages are virtually unknown in our culture. There are no marriages where one spouse obeys the other spouse in every area of their lives. Typically, one spouse is in charge of certain areas of endeavor, while the other spouse takes control of others. For example, the wife takes care of the children while the husband works. The wife might focus exclusively on the home and the children, and the husband may be totally absorbed by his work. Over the years, the spouses may find that they have less and less in common with each other. They will not vie for equal power and therefore will not fight with each other, but they may become distant and uninvolved. When they change to a different arrangement—for example, as the children grow older, the wife goes back to school or to work—they may begin to argue with each other as the relationship becomes more symmetrical.

The word *symmetrical* was first introduced by anthropologist Gregory Bateson in his work on primitive tribes in New Guinea.[5] He observed that the warriors of one tribe would suddenly rush to the camp of another tribe and shake their spears and shout curses at their neighbors. Later, the members of the other tribe might retaliate in the same way, or they might hold a special ceremony communicating with the gods, demonstrating in this way that they were better than the other tribe. According to Bateson, the primary message in this behavior appears to be "I am as good as you are." Obviously, the danger in this type of behavior is that it can escalate until the only solution is for the parties to actually engage in battle.

Symmetrical behavior is a competitive pattern that is the opposite of collaborative behavior and often leads to power struggles. Taking turns and sharing are essential aspects of complementary relationships. In cultures that have well-defined roles for male and female, the areas in which competition can occur are relatively limited. In our culture, financial challenges, affluence, mobility, and sexual equality have led to a general loosening of role definition, leaving many more arenas in which power struggles can occur—we call this symmetrical escalation.

In marriage, symmetrical escalation usually takes the form of arguing and bickering that indicate one partner's fear of being inferior—that is, fear that the spouse does not consider the partner an equal. In such struggles, each spouse is trying to persuade, maneuver, or battle the other spouse into concluding, "My spouse is my equal, or my spouse may even be better than me." These struggles can be initiated by something as simple as an offhand remark.

Let's look at a conversation that took place between Amy and Jason in an Italian restaurant in New York City:

Jason: This is a great restaurant for pasta. You should order pasta.

Amy: I feel like eating a steak.

Jason: Why would you come to an Italian restaurant to order steak?! Get the ravioli—I've had them before, they're delicious.

Amy: No, thank you, I feel like steak.

Jason: You're missing out totally on this restaurant if you don't order pasta.

Amy: I appreciate your advice, but I want steak.

Jason: I'm not giving you advice. I'm telling you an obvious fact.

Amy: You are giving me advice, and I don't need it. Can I order my steak, or do I have to order chicken?

Jason: Order whatever the f*** you want.

(The meal is spent in angry silence as each feels that the other has ruined the outing.)

In most cases, spouses are not aware of their symmetrical escalation, nor do they realize that the subject of the argument makes no difference. The spouses may be discussing what candidate to vote for, what car to buy, whether to send the children to private school, or what is the most efficient method of cleaning the toilet. To a certain extent symmetrical escalation is inevitable in the course of a marriage, but some couples are in such a malignant struggle that they cannot even agree to divorce.

Dolores and Martin had been married for 20 years. They invited some new friends over for dinner. When their friends commented on what a nice home they had and said that it probably reflected how good their relationship must be, Dolores said, "Not at all. We have a horrible relationship. We don't divorce only because neither one of us wants to have custody of the children."

Although this was said in humor, a couple can be so focused on their power struggle that they will even reject their own children to prove a point. In some couples the struggle is over who is more competent, or kind, or knowledgeable. In others it becomes about who is meaner and more abusive. When this happens, it is called malignant escalation.

Malignant escalation often includes intimidating or threatening behavior. As the spouses vie for power, they might threaten infidelity, divorce, or violence. Relatives, co-workers in a family-owned business, even children might be used in the struggle, as with Dolores and Martin. Often a couple's power struggle is carried over to a family-owned business (which make up 80 percent of the businesses in the United States). A couple can lose sight of the common goal of succeeding in business or of raising good children as their vision becomes narrower and narrower because of their focus on their marital power struggle.

Power struggles occur in many relationships, not only in marriage. They can happen between siblings, between parent and child, and between friends and co-workers. When power struggles are occurring at the management level of a company, they tend to repeat at the lower levels. When you notice power struggles at the lower levels of your organization, it's time to think about who is involved in this type of struggle at the upper levels. The best way of resolving conflicts at the lower levels is to resolve them at the upper levels.

We can use the technique of setting aside a unique time and place to mitigate power struggles in all our relationships, whether with spouses, children, parents, friends, or co-workers. Set a special day, time, and place that will be devoted to discussing issues and areas of disagreement. This is an executive meeting of sorts that can take place at a restaurant or any other public place. It is best to keep it away from the home or workplace—the site of the struggle.

Let's say the meeting will take place regularly on Thursday nights at the local Chinese restaurant. During this meeting each participant will take turns voicing all of their criticisms and disagreements. At no time during the week will you engage in criticizing or complaining or in responding to anyone else's criticisms or complaints. Instead, keep a notebook in which you jot down whatever troubles you want to discuss at the special meeting. During the meeting, be careful to listen, understand, and respond to each participant's issues. Be sure to reserve the last few minutes for pleasant conversation to ensure that the meeting ends with a good feeling. In this way, power struggles and unpleasant conversations are kept from invading the entire relationship.

Relighting the Fire

Margaret and Carl had been married for 30 years but were about to get a divorce. A disagreement about money had been the last straw. As Margaret put it, "We have a terminal relationship. I think the only thing that keeps the marriage together is money. There is no love." When I inquired about what she meant in terms of money, I was a bit taken aback by her response. Both Carl and Margaret worked. Carl gave Margaret all the money he made and so provided for the family. Out of this money, Margaret gave Carl an allowance. But Margaret kept all the money that she made and spent it on herself.

Over the years, as their daughters became adults, the couple had become distant from each other to the point that they had not had sexual relations for 3 years. Carl had held a government job for most of his life, and now he was ready to retire. As his wife, Margaret had to sign papers so that he could withdraw his retirement money. She refused to do so. This was the last straw for Carl. Margaret was not only the expert and the one who had power over everything having to do with money, now she wanted power over his retirement also. From Margaret's point of view, she said, "If we decide not to divorce, then naturally I will go ahead and sign." If they divorced, she wanted the house and half of his retirement.

I knew that the money issue could not be solved unless I first revived the passion in the marriage. So I asked Margaret, "Do you remember when he first swept you off your feet?"

I deliberately phrased the question so that it would have romantic and sexual connotations. I wanted to see whether there was a spark still there that could be fanned into flame. Margaret remembered that she had met Carl at a dance. "A girlfriend of mine introduced us when I arrived. He said, 'Have we met before?' I said, 'I was wondering the same thing.' He looked pretty good to me, so we talked."

"Was that the night when he swept you off your feet?" I asked.

Margaret went on, "When I finally convinced him that I couldn't go out with him that night because of my girlfriend, he put his arm around me, and it was an electric arm." She laughed, and Carl smiled affectionately. "That was when I knew," said Margaret. "I had dated other guys before, but I never felt that, whatever it was, when he just put his arm around me. And then he said (she made a deep voice), 'I'll see you tomorrow then.'"

Listening to Margaret, I knew that there was still a spark of the old passion that had brought Margaret and Carl together. I knew that it would be easier to change the relationship through Margaret. She was more energetic and less frustrated than Carl.

I asked Carl to leave the room for a few minutes because I wanted to talk with Margaret alone. I said to her, "I'm worried because I can see that you chose a great husband who has been supportive of you in so many ways—financially, emotionally, with the children. I'm worried that some other woman, not nearly as deserving as yourself, is going to snatch him."

"I know," she said. "My friends have told me that."

"The problem for you," I said, "is how to bring back that affection, that desire, the way he put his arm. . . ."

She interrupted: "Maybe I could start by cooking something that he likes. I never cook for him."

I talked to her about how she could surprise him the next day with a candlelight dinner and insisted she should be wearing nothing but a negligee.

I said, "I have no doubt that he loves you. But would you know how to seduce him?"

"I think I could," said Margaret. "But what would there be in that for me?"

"His electricity again."

"His electricity is not there."

"I think you could use your charms to arouse that arm again," I said.

"We haven't had sex for so long that I'm worried that he's had an affair with another woman, and then I think about AIDS," she said.

"So go to the pharmacy and buy six different color condoms. Towards the end of the dinner, you take out the condoms and ask him, 'What is your favorite color? Pick one.'"

Margaret laughed. "That will certainly surprise him."

When I saw them a week later, Carl said, "The day after we met you, I walked into the house, and I thought, 'Am I in the right house? Is this the Margaret I know?'"

The candlelight dinner was a big success, and Margaret had no problem turning on his electricity again. I pointed out that she was an expert at seduction and electricity. A few days later she signed the retirement papers. They met with me one more time and planned how they would have a big party to renew their marital vows and they would go on a second honeymoon.

Margaret was able to relinquish some of her control over the money because now she felt she had some control over their sexuality, and she was getting the love that she truly needed. Margaret and Carl were now complementing each other in a happy way.

We can change symmetrical relationships to complementary by nurturing the sexual polarity in our relationships. By allowing yourself to cultivate and express your feminine or your masculine nature, you can create the complementarity that is essential for mutual attraction.

The Power of Networks

Recently we have witnessed how the US economy, based on hierarchical structures, fell into disarray. Rising in its place was the new information economy, in which greater flexibility was necessary and hierarchies were inappropriate. A new networking model evolved.

Networking is a process that links clusters of people. A powerful tool for social action, it has been responsible for the evolution of the women's movement, as well as the many consumer organizations and various other networks, including those for food distribution, environmental protection, education, and information. Networks offer the horizontal link, the egalitarian relationship that most of us crave if we take seriously the ideology of democracy. Hierarchies are about power and control. Networks are about empowering and nurturing.[6]

I thought about my work as a therapist and found that it coincided with these changes in the culture. I had made a transition in my thinking and in my focus of intervention from hierarchies to networks.

I was always puzzled by how seemingly powerful and competent adults could be such helpless and incompetent parents. And I was even more interested in how little children, apparently helpless, could be powerful helpers in the family. I noticed that although the family appears to be a traditional hierarchical organization, with parents in charge of the children, sometimes this is not the case. How often does a parent side with a child to help the other parent or to isolate the other parent? How many children help their parents' marriage stay together? How many children succeed in separating their parents? These and many similar questions led me to think that perhaps organizing a family in a hierarchical model is not necessarily the best idea.

I developed a new model of networks where the communication style is lateral, diagonal, and from the bottom up. The stories below show how it has worked with various families. Siblings can help each other; uncles and aunts, cousins, and friends are important resources; children can help their parents to change. A network is like a fishnet, where the nodes are all linked together in a three-dimensional structure. The family is a self-help network. Here are some examples of how it functions.

Sisterhood Is Powerful

Allison suffered from anxiety attacks that she thought were related to conflicts with her lover. She confided in her sister, Monica, but Monica knew that the root cause of Allison's anxiety was something quite different. Allison had three adult sons who had disappeared from her life and did not write or call. She did not know whether they were dead or alive. Allison lived with her daughter, who was an alcoholic.

Monica decided to take action. She contacted Allison's estranged ex-husband, friends, relatives, and the police. The sons were found. Monica organized a coming together at Allison's home. She prepared the sons for reconciliation with their mother and their sister. The meeting was a success, and communication was resumed. Allison recovered from her anxiety attacks, and her daughter found a boyfriend and learned to control her alcoholism.

The damaging effects of family estrangement cannot be underestimated. Sometimes all it takes is the effort of one family member to put the network back together and heal its members.

A Positive Penalty

People in a family can help each other in indirect ways and even outside of their awareness. Sandra consulted with me because she had a serious problem of procrastinating with writing her dissertation. She constantly found excuses for writing things other than her thesis. This was not difficult to do because she worked as a journalist.

I sympathized with her problem and asked her about her family, her friends, how she got along with her siblings, and so on. Sandra said that she had a stepsister in Europe whom she disliked intensely. I changed the subject back to her dissertation and asked how many pages a day she reasonably could expect to write. She said she could write four pages. I told Sandra that there was a solution to her problem, but first she had to promise that she would follow my directive. She was not going to like it, I said, and I was not going to argue with her. She knew how important it was to obtain her PhD degree and further her career, so she accepted my decision.

I said, "Every day that you don't write four pages, I want you to write a $100 check to your stepsister and mail it to her with a note saying, 'With all my love' or 'Thinking about you.'"

Sandra said that was the last thing in the world she wanted to do and immediately began to negotiate exceptions. I agreed that if there were an international crisis and she had to fly somewhere to report it, that would not count. She was not expected to write on the airplane or while reporting. But the rest of the time, she was on the honor system.

Sandra finished her dissertation within a few months, and the sister never got a check. However, once the dissertation was finished, Sandra, intrigued by my directive, visited her stepsister in Europe, and they became friends. Sandra not only finished her dissertation but also recovered her relationship with her stepsister.

Chapter 5

ARE YOU REALLY SAYING WHAT YOU THINK YOU'RE SAYING?

We communicate through everything we do and everything we do not do, through words as well as through silence. The tone of voice and the body posture, the gesture and the gaze all communicate. We cannot avoid communicating any more than we can avoid breathing. Often what is not said is more powerful than what is actually verbalized. As the French psychiatrist Jacques Lacan wrote, "It is the absence of the warm gesture that defines the coldness of the relationship."[1]

Communication can be digital or analogical. In digital communication, each message has only one referent and consists of arbitrary signs. The word *table*, for example, bears no resemblance to the specific object it denotes and has no meaning other than that of a sign used to refer to a certain piece of furniture. From the point of view of digital communication, a headache, for example, is just a pain in the head and nothing else.

Analogue communication has more than one referent, and an analogical message resembles the object it denotes. The clenched fist is both a sign for a certain type of behavior and an example of that behavior. In contrast to digital communication, analogical communication can express different magnitudes. For example, crying, screaming, and banging one's head against the wall are actions that analogically express different magnitudes of despair.

An analogue message can be assigned meaning only when one takes into account a context of other messages. From the point of view of analogical communication, a headache not only is a pain in the head but also may be an expression of worry, an indication of dislike, a way of declining a task or refusing to be involved, or a request for affection. The meaning assigned to the headache as an analogical message will depend on the situation and the context of other communication during which the analogical message takes place.

Experiences and behaviors can be conceptualized as either digital or analogue. A person's headaches can be described as an event with no other reference than a pain in the head. This is a digital description. Or we can describe it as an analogue with more than one referent. When a person is talking about his headaches, he is talking about more than one kind of pain. From this point of view, behavior is always communication on many levels.[2]

Meaning Changes Depending on Your View of Unit, Sequence, and Hierarchy

Our understanding of a situation will vary depending on the information we take into account. The three most important points of view that affect the meaning we attribute to events are unit, sequence, and hierarchy. In understanding the wolf, will we look at the behavior of a single animal or at the behavior of the pack? Will we predict the behavior of a hurricane as it lands on the shores of the Caribbean or as it originates in Africa? How much of the behavior of a child is contingent on the wishes of the parent? In all these instances, our conclusions are determined by what unit, sequence, and hierarchy we take into account.

Let's look at a deceptively simple situation. A boy is sitting with his parents in the waiting room of a psychologist. The boy begins to tap his fingers on a table. The father says, "Don't do that." The mother says, "Leave him alone." The boy sits quietly. The father says, "How come you're so quiet?" The mother says, "You're always picking on him."

There is nothing that the boy can do to escape this **sequence** of interaction. Even if he does nothing, the sequence will repeat. If you look at the situation from the point of view of a **unit of one**, you might think that the boy is hyperactive or oppositional. If you take into account a **unit of two** involving the boy and the father, you might think that the father is overly involved with the child in a negative way. If you take into account a **unit of two** involving the boy and the mother, you might think that the mother is overly involved with the boy in an overly protective way. If you take into account a **unit of three**, you realize that the boy is caught in a disagreement between the parents who have different views on how he should behave.

If you then consider **hierarchy**, you realize that the child is dependent on the parents for physical and emotional support. He cannot leave. Whereas an adult can physically go away from an unpleasant situation with the parents, a child cannot. The child is caught in a hierarchy where he is receiving contradictory messages.

Just as it is impossible to understand the behavior of the bee without looking at the hive, so it is impossible to truly understand the behavior of the individual without looking at the system of interaction. It is also difficult to establish what starts the sequence and what ends it. It can also be hard to tell who is truly in control. Apparently, the master is in a superior position to the servant, but often the master is so dependent on the servant that the servant is truly in charge. This is not to say that there is not real power the rich have over the poor or the oppressor over the oppressed. Yet without a servant, there is no master, and without a subject, there is no tyrant.

Here is another example of the complexities of unit, sequence, and hierarchy in social systems.

Who's Picking On Whom?

Mandy and her husband Joe are having lunch at a restaurant with Joe's mother, Gloria, celebrating Mother's Day. Gloria says, "Joe, dear, when are you going to get a promotion?" Mandy speaks before Joe can reply, "Gloria, don't pick on Joe. He works very hard and makes very good money." Gloria says, "I'm not picking on him. I just think he's capable of doing better." Joe says, "Mandy, she was just asking me a question. She wasn't picking on me."

A few minutes go by in silence, and then the two women talk about the food. After a while, Gloria says, "Joe, you seem awfully quiet today. Are you worried about something?" Mandy says, "He's just enjoying his food. He's not worried about anything." Gloria says, "I didn't mean to be critical. I just think he's very quiet today." Joe says, "Mandy, she was just asking an innocent question." After a while, Gloria decides to bring up a safe subject. She says, "Joe, it's great to see you eating pasta. You've always been such a meat-and-potatoes person." Mandy says, "That's not true. He loves pasta, he eats it all the time." Gloria says, "Oh, I didn't know that." Joe says, "Mandy, you know very well that I only started eating pasta a few weeks ago."

If you look at this situation in terms of a unit of one, you would think that Mandy is critical of her mother-in-law, or that Joe is critical of Mandy, or that Gloria defends herself. If you have a unit of two, you might think that Joe and Mandy disagree about his mother. If you have a unit of three, you will see that they are caught in a repetitive pattern: Gloria asks Joe something, Mandy interrupts to defend him, Gloria becomes defensive, and Joe criticizes Mandy. If you assess the relationship's hierarchy, you would observe that Gloria is in a superior position to Joe as his mother and therefore feels entitled to ask personal questions and make personal comments. You will also notice that Gloria and Joe seem to be in a cross-generational coalition against Mandy.

Metaphoric Communication

A child who says, "My stomach hurts," may be referring to more than one kind of pain, and she may also be referring to the pain of another person. For example, she might be saying that her mother is suffering. A message may have a second referent, a second meaning, which may refer to someone other than the person expressing the message.

Just as a message may have a second referent, so may a sequence of interaction. That is, a sequence of interaction between two people may be a metaphor for and take the place of a different sequence of interaction between two other people. For example, a father comes home from work upset, worried, and anxious because he fears he will be fired or he has had a dispute with his boss. As his wife reassures him and comforts him, their son develops an asthma attack. The father then begins to comfort and reassure the son in the same way that the wife had been comforting and reassuring him. The interaction between father and son replaces and is a metaphor for the interaction between wife and husband. At the time that the father is reassuring the child, the wife cannot be reassuring the husband. One sequence has replaced the other.

In any family, there will be variations in who is the focus of any sequence of interaction. Sometimes, a sequence may focus on the husband's work difficulties, sometimes on the symptoms of a child, sometimes on problems with an in-law, or on money difficulties. But the sequence of interaction will remain the same. For instance, there might always be someone helpless, who exhibits involuntary behavior, and someone helpful, who fails to help. This sequence might appear in various ways in a family and may involve various dyads, with each sequence representing metaphorically another sequence.[3]

Trouble in Bed

Iris was married to Jacob, a handsome businessman. She often noticed that he was looking at other women and suspected he was unfaithful to her. She would interrogate him on the phone during the day about where he was, with whom, and what was he doing. When he came home in the evening, the questioning would continue. The fact was that there were several signs of infidelity, and Iris had good reason to be suspicious.

Sam, their 5-year-old son, began to wet the bed, something he hadn't done since he was 3 years old. Iris and Jacob became very worried about this behavior and found a new closeness with each other as they consulted with different specialists and tried different methods of helping Sam.

Sam's bad behavior in bed was a metaphor for Jacob's bad behavior in other women's beds. The interaction around Sam's bed-wetting had replaced the interaction around Jacob's possible infidelities and had brought the couple together in their concern for their son.

Some months went by, and Iris's mother became ill. Iris began to spend most of her time with her mother, keeping her company, taking care of her, and visiting doctors. Jacob complained that Iris should be taking care of her own family and was upset about how Iris was neglecting him and Sam. The focus of interaction had now shifted to what Iris was doing wrong. Iris's behavior toward her mother and Jacob's objections were a metaphor for Sam's and Jacob's behavior in bed and had replaced those concerns. The pattern that repeated was that someone did something wrong, and the other two were concerned about him or her. Eventually, Iris's mother's health improved, and Iris went back to her concerns about Jacob's possible infidelities.

People can be caught in these repetitive patterns for years and years.

The metaphors in sequences of interactions are quite different than metaphors in a dream or in a symbol—a different order of concepts is involved when we talk about the metaphoric aspects of sequences of behavior.

We can choose to focus on concrete facts, observations, and information, or we can be interested in covert, implied, or indirect references. As we saw in the story of Susan in Chapter 4, a child's refusal to go to school may be viewed as disobedience, with the resulting focus on how to get him back in school. In contrast, his refusal to go to school may be considered an allusion to his mother's refusal to go to work and to the pressure his father puts on her about it. The child's refusal to go to school in spite of his parents' efforts may be considered an allusion to and a metaphor for his mother's conflict with his father. The parents' struggle with the child may have replaced the struggle between the parents. It follows logically that if the husband stops pressuring the wife to go to work, the child might begin to go to school. Changing one sequence of interaction may have repercussions on other sequences in a family. The same applies to relationships in all kinds of organizations.

Metaphors have several functions. The first is to communicate: A son's violence, for example, may be expressing his mother's rage. A second function is to displace: A mother's frustration with her son may be a metaphor for her frustration with her husband, and may replace that frustration. A third function is to promote closeness and attach people to one another: A quarrel between father and daughter may be a metaphor for the resentments between husband and wife, which are expressed only through the daughter, in this way bringing the spouses together. A fourth function is to punish and gain revenge: A son of divorced parents may become delinquent and so punish the father for leaving the family as well as provide revenge for the mother, who can blame the father's abandonment for the boy's delinquency. When communication is metaphorical, problems are difficult to resolve because messages do not refer to what they ostensibly refer to and people can become caught in endless repetitive sequences.

Communication can be straightforward or paradoxical. A straightforward message is "Listen to me." A paradoxical message is "Don't listen to me." A communication is paradoxical when it involves two messages that qualify each other in conflicting ways. The messages "Be spontaneous," "Don't be so obedient," and "I want you to dominate me" are common paradoxes in human relationships. They are paradoxical because if the receiver of the message complies with the request, he is not complying with the request. The paradox occurs because one directive is qualified by another, at a different level of abstraction, in a conflicting way.[4]

What Depression?

Charles, a 60-year-old accountant, came to see me about his feelings of depression. Due to his "depression," he neglected his work to the point that he hadn't even paid his own taxes for 3 years. Laura, his wife of 30 years, was a kind woman who was very concerned about him. When the children left home, she had gone back to school and had recently become a therapist. Laura constantly tried to help Charles with his "depression," and in that sense, he had almost become her patient. Charles behaved helplessly, while Laura was competent, understanding, and always trying to cheer him up, even though she was exasperated with him.

I suggested to Charles that he should try something new. Three times a week he would pretend to be depressed, and Laura would have to figure out whether he was really depressed or he was pretending. My idea was that if Laura didn't know whether Charles was really depressed or just pretending, she would not respond to him in her usual kind, understanding way, and their pattern of behaving like doctor and patient would be broken. I asked Charles to practice by pretending to be depressed in my presence, and I asked Laura to comment on whether he was doing it right. Charles had difficulty pretending to be depressed, and Laura criticized his tone of voice, his body posture, and his choice of words. Charles became annoyed at this exercise and said that perhaps he was not depressed—he was just irresponsible about his work. He suddenly saw that his depression was, in fact, an excuse for being lazy and procrastinating. I said I couldn't agree more. In the next few weeks he caught up with his work and did not complain about depression again.

There Are Irrational Aspects to Every Relationship

If we were rational beings, we would always seek to avoid pain and to experience pleasure. But we are seldom rational where relationships are concerned. Why is it that some men always fall in love with women who reject them or treat them with cruelty? Why is it that some women stay attached to men who abuse them repeatedly and are only able to leave them when the abuse has stopped? Why do some people work for someone they despise?

How can one explain that the most intelligent, gifted people in the world so often have the worst private lives and the worst relationships?

The answer is: love, fear, insecurity, and familiarity. These are the powerful emotions that keep us chained to a life we don't want to live. The man who falls in love with rejecting women probably had a rejecting mother, so he is familiar with the experience of being rejected. A rejecting woman gives him pain, but she also gives him the security of what is familiar. He's had that experience before; he knows what to expect. A world of non-rejection would be unfamiliar and would arouse fear of the unknown. A rejecting woman, similar to the mother, is known and predictable.

A woman is attached to a man who abuses her. Maybe she loves him—love is more powerful than pain. Certainly she fears him. Fear is the most blinding of all the emotions. She forgets her civil rights and only remembers them after the abuse has stopped. She doesn't believe in the possibility of freedom. Maybe she believes she is unworthy and deserves the violence. Perhaps because of her past, violence is something she is familiar with, so it gives her certainty. The violence also gives her a sense of self-righteousness. She is the victim, not the criminal. In spite of it all, she loves. This makes her feel superior and gives her a sense of significance.

Most parents love their babies, who eventually grow into children. The children grow into adults, who sometimes become mean and ungrateful. Many parents keep giving, behaving as if these adults were still babies, ignoring the fact that the more they give, the worse they will be treated. Why do some parents never learn? Perhaps for some people the experience of giving birth, of caring for an infant and a child is so powerful that it becomes the essence of the emotion of love and the experience of familiarity. They are certain of their love. It defines their identity. They are the love givers. The parent gives and the child takes. No amount of hostility and lack of gratitude deters the parent from giving, because giving has become their certainty.

Some of the most intelligent people so often have troubled relationships because love, fear, and uncertainty can overpower the intelligent mind. Intelligence alone doesn't conquer these emotions. What is required is wisdom.

Another irrational aspect of relationships is that so often what comes out of our mouths is not what is in our hearts or in our heads. Often we speak what we don't intend to say. A mother loves her child, yet when she speaks, every word seems to be critical of the child. A lover wants to demonstrate affection, but the words that come out are arrogant and cold. Many times we express the opposite of what we would like to convey. This often happens when our needs are not fulfilled.

Weapons We Use When Our Needs Are Not Being Fulfilled

Let's look again at Jenn and Paul. What weapons did they use against each other? Jenn was very skillful with words and had a great sense of humor, but her humor often turned biting and became a weapon that she used to put down Paul. Her humor was often experienced by Paul as sarcasm and her teasing as criticism. Jenn was much more verbal than Paul and often interrupted him, spoke for him, or didn't give him the time to express himself. Her speaking for him and her impatience also made Paul feel small and insignificant.

Paul's main weapon was simply the threat of leaving the marriage.

If they were going to save their marriage, Paul and Jenn had to recognize the weapons they were using to hurt one another and cease to use them.

Sarcasm is one of the most destructive of weapons. It uses humor, a good quality, to make someone else feel small. The same goes for teasing—a very little goes a very long way. Humor, sarcasm, and teasing are subtle weapons. Unlike anger, violence, and threats, they initially may appear benign, but over time they are as destructive as more obvious weapons.

Criticism

Criticism calls attention to a person's defects and often becomes a self-fulfilling prophecy. It is best to point out the good qualities rather than the bad, unless you deliberately want to bring out the other person's defects. When you bring out defects, you are creating them by calling the person's attention to what is negative.

Some parents are overwhelmingly critical of their children, making constant remarks such as "Don't act silly," "You're talking too loud," "You will never be good at sports," "I can imagine what your report card is going to look like," "You smell," and "That's a stupid thing to say." Over time the long-suffering child incorporates these statements and grows to believe that he or she is silly, loud, bad at sports and at school, smelly, and stupid.

Some people not only are critical of their children but also can get in the habit of making critical remarks about their spouse. Common criticisms in marital relationships are "You're a slob," "You're too rigid," "You're so boring," "You can't even keep a clean house," "You don't make enough money," and on and on. Even though these remarks rarely lead to change, they continue to be made thoughtlessly and from habit.

If you are guilty of being excessively critical, change is difficult but always possible. Once you make the decision to stop being critical, tell your spouse and your children that you have made this decision. Then buy a piggy bank and place it in the living room. Every time you catch yourself making a critical remark, put a dollar in the piggy bank. When the piggy bank is full, buy a gift for your spouse and/or for your children. The interesting thing about this strategy is that your family might begin to provoke you and taunt you so that you will be critical and they will get their gifts.

Your problem may not be that you are the victim of your spouse's criticism. If that is the case, chances are that you are sustaining his or her criticism by the way you respond. You may become angry or hurt, or you may respond with criticism or hostility. Chances are that your spouse is pushing your buttons, and soon you are involved in a malignant escalation. You are reactive, and your reaction brings on more criticism. You need to try something completely different. You may want to simply say, "Oh, dear!" And to each criticism add another "dear." Soon you might be saying, "Oh, dear, dear, dear, and dear!" You might go about your business or continue the conversation as if you had not heard the criticism. You might even choose to take off an item of clothing with each criticism until you end up stark naked!

Generosity

Even generosity can be used as a weapon. Generosity can breed resentment. The generous act defines the giver as morally superior, thus automatically defining the receiver as inferior because he or she is in a position of needing the generosity of the giver. So the receiver can become resentful. The resentful person cannot be happy. The best way to counter feelings of resentment is through the regular practice of gratitude. Martin Seligman, PhD, an expert in the field of positive psychology, has demonstrated that gratitude is conducive to happiness.[5] He gave subjects a simple test that measured their level of happiness. Then he asked them to think of one person to whom they were grateful. It could be a relative, a teacher, a friend, and so forth.

Then they were to write a letter to this person expressing all their gratitude, and they would deliver the letter in person and read it to the recipient. After this, their level of happiness was measured again and showed a significant increase as compared to a control group that was not asked to write the letter.

Indirect Influence

In order to be able to make our own decisions, we need to understand how we might be under the indirect influence of others who may have programmed us in the past or who might even be programming us now. But we don't have to allow the programming from our past to control our present and our future. We are also programmers of others, influencing them in terms of their focus, the meaning they give to experience, and what they can do to obtain what they want. Most of the time we program others unwittingly, but we can also do so deliberately.

We constantly try to preserve our inner world—our sense of identity—and we use certain defense mechanisms in order to do so. For example, denial: "I am not a drug addict. I use drugs occasionally." Another defense is projection: "I'm not angry—you are." The mechanism of regression: "I'm going to cry like a baby." These are some of the operations we use to protect ourselves from others and to maintain the sense of who we think we are.

We also act on the inner worlds of others in order to preserve our own inner world. We do so by using what the British psychiatrist R. D. Laing called transpersonal defenses and we call indirect influence: the attempt to regulate the inner life of another person in order to preserve our own.[6]

One way to get someone to do what one wants is to give an order. To get someone to be what one wants him to be is a different matter. The hypnotist doesn't tell the subject what to be; he tells her what she is. Such attributions are often more powerful than orders, coercion, or persuasion. It is possible that our earliest instructions are in the form of attributions. A man is told he is a bad or a good boy, not instructed to be one. The mode for this type of communication is probably nonverbal.

Hypnosis is an experimental model of a naturally occurring phenomenon in families. The hypnotist instructs the subject, and part of the instruction is not to know that he has been instructed. The same happens in families. A mother instructs a child to feel sad, and part of the instruction is not to know that she has been instructed. A simple way to do this is to just tell the person what they feel, as in "You are angry." Better yet is to tell a third party, in front of the person, what the person feels. How much of who we are is what we have been hypnotized to be?

The hypnotist doesn't say, "I order you to feel cold." He says, "It is cold." The subject immediately feels cold. Many children begin life like this, experiencing what their parents experience, or what the parents want them to experience. Soon they learn to use the same operation on others. So a husband may say to his wife, "I know you are full of anger," and he knows he is right even though anger may not be what she is experiencing. In ongoing relationships it soon becomes unnecessary to even say anything. A glance, a touch, a cough is an instruction.

When parents say of a child that he has attention deficit disorder, they are instructing the child to not pay attention. When a wife says that her husband is insensitive, she is instructing him to be insensitive. The difference with hypnosis is that the hypnotist knows what he is doing; family members usually don't.

"I try to help him make friends, but he is so shy." "She never stands still." "He never listens."

Statements made by parents about their children, no matter how apparently well-meaning or supportive, can have pernicious effects and only reinforce unwanted behavior.

Induction

Suppose, like Jenn, I project my father onto my husband. Or, like Paul, I project my mother and sisters onto my wife. My husband becomes like my father to me. My wife becomes like my mother. I may or may not succeed in inducing him to be like my father. The act of inducing him to embody my projection of my father is what we call induction. Induction is one person projecting something onto the other's experience. Through induction I can maneuver my husband into such a position that he begins to act and even to feel like my father. He can begin to feel and to act like my father without even having met him. Such inductions are going on all the time.

The conversation below, between a mother and her 14-year-old daughter, illustrates the principle of induction.

Mother: You are evil.

Daughter: No, I'm not.

Mother: Yes, you are.

Daughter: Uncle Jack doesn't think so.

Mother: He doesn't love you as I do. Only a mother knows the truth about her daughter, and only one who loves you as I do will ever tell you the truth about yourself, no matter what it is. If you don't believe me, just look at yourself in the mirror carefully, and you will see that I'm telling the truth.

Obviously, this is an extreme, even disturbing, example. But suppose we change one word, as Laing suggests: Replace "evil" with "pretty."

Mother: You are pretty.

Daughter: No, I'm not.

Mother: Yes, you are.

Daughter: Uncle Jack doesn't think so.

Mother: He doesn't love you as I do. Only a mother knows the truth about her daughter, and only one who loves you as I do will ever tell you the truth about yourself, no matter what it is. If you don't believe me, just look at yourself in the mirror carefully, and you will see that I'm telling the truth.

Whether the attribution is evil, pretty, ugly, or good, the structure of the induction is identical. This induction is so common that we only notice it when it is disturbing. We all employ similar versions of this technique, and we may well justify them, but it is important to reflect on the structure of the induction, not only the content.

When we try to induce a child or lover to feel positively about himself, it is appropriate and good. When we induce someone to feel negative, it is disturbing and destructive. The root of all violence in the world is negative induction: projecting negative values such as "evil" or "dangerous" on other individuals, groups, or nations. It is also the root of much suffering.[7]

Negative Projection

Gonzalo, the oldest son of an upper-class Spanish family, was sent to a boarding school run by the Opus Dei, the most conservative branch of the Catholic Church. He was made to cut himself until he bled as punishment for his sins, a sin being any impure thought or just the fact of existing. He was to do this in private, and the priests would just ask to see the scars. He lived in fear and self-hatred. Later in life he became a successful entrepreneur—handsome, intelligent, cultured, and worldly.

Yet he was plagued by panic attacks and self-loathing that were totally obsolete. The fear and the self-hatred that the priests had induced in him as a child had become so entrenched in his identity that he couldn't let go.

The Power of Expectations

We are all familiar with how we can provoke a certain response and bring out the best or the worst in the other person. What is not so obvious is that sometimes simply our expectation of how the other will behave elicits precisely that behavior, even though it might be the behavior we wish the other would not indulge in.

When we ask for something with the expectation that it won't happen, chances are, it won't. For example, when a man approaches a woman for a date, expecting that she'll say no, chances are, she will. When we ask for a raise, expecting that it won't happen, chances are, it won't. If we expect our children to do poorly in school, we increase the chances that they will fail.

There was a time when scientists believed that they could stand away from their data and observe it objectively in a nonbiased way and without influencing the data they were observing. It was also believed that the experimenter, while manipulating the subjects of his experiment, was detached from the subjects and able to refrain from influencing them either deliberately or outside of his awareness. A series of experiments demonstrated that no such thing is possible.

In the 1960s, Robert Rosenthal, a professor at the University of California, became interested in how a person's expectations can influence others. He was fascinated by the idea that one person's expectation for the behavior of another can come to serve as a self-fulfilling prophecy. In a groundbreaking experiment, he told elementary school teachers that certain children in the classroom were more intelligent than the rest. But, in fact, those children were selected at random. By the end of the year, those children scored higher than the rest in intelligence and achievement tests.[8]

This experiment fundamentally changed the way we view relationships, the way we view scientific experiments, and, for that matter, the way we view any observer of living things.

Rosenthal's experiment with schoolchildren was replicated with rats. Psychologists who worked with rats in a lab were told that certain rats were more intelligent than others. The rats had been picked at random, yet those that the psychologists believed to be more intelligent solved mazes and performed tasks significantly more competently than the other rats. The teachers in the classroom and the psychologists in the lab unwittingly influenced their subjects in the direction of their expectations.

These studies were replicated many times with similar results. It was found that when coaches are led to expect better athletic performance from their athletes, they tend to get it. And when behavioral researchers are led to expect certain responses from their research participants, they tend to get those responses. There is no such thing as an objective observer. When our subjects are living creatures, we influence them as we observe them. It follows logically that when we are facing a challenge involving human beings, we cannot look at the way people behave without taking our own motives, inclinations, and perceptions into account. We are constantly influencing the behaviors and interactions that we are observing. In that sense, we are part of the problem we are trying to solve.

Rosenthal became interested in nonverbal communication when he realized that the mechanisms by which interpersonal expectations are communicated are largely nonverbal. That is, when people expect more of those with whom they come in contact, they treat them differently in nonverbal ways. In some of his most recent research, he took silent videos or tone-of-voice clips of about 30 seconds or less from lectures given by college instructors. He was able to predict, using 30 seconds of instructors' nonverbal behavior, the end-of-term ratings college students would give their instructors.

In other research, Rosenthal took brief segments of doctors' interactions with patients and showed that we can predict which doctors are more likely to be sued by which patients. He also found that jury verdicts can often be predicted from the nonverbal behavior of the judges as they instruct the jury.[9]

On the one hand, we know that there is an objective reality. There are people with their own motivations, thoughts, feelings, and behaviors. On the other hand, we are constantly modifying the motivations, thoughts, feelings, and behaviors of those other people. We cannot help influencing those we interact with, and we influence them not only through our deliberately planned behavior but even just through expectations that we might convey nonverbally.[10]

A Swiss psychologist told me about a great intervention he made to help an 8-year-old boy to go from being the worst in his class to becoming the best. He asked the teacher to "loan" the boy some A's, that is, to give him A's that he didn't deserve. The boy would have to pay back the A's with interest, that is, he would have to get A-pluses that he actually deserved. The loaned A's were a sign of the high expectations that the teacher had for this child. In addition, the idea of paying back with interest was consistent with the culture of banking that is so prevalent in Switzerland and took advantage of the fact that the boy's father, whom he admired, was an economist. As a result of the teacher's intervention, the boy felt a special connection with her as well as with his banker father. He applied himself and was soon earning A's.

Some people go through life with a consistent set of negative expectations about themselves—"People don't like me," "I will be rejected," "I have no energy," "I won't succeed." It is difficult to give up lifelong negative expectations because in many ways they are comforting. If you know you will fail, you don't need to try, so you don't have to make the effort. It can also be comforting, and in some sense rewarding, to indulge in food, alcohol, and other addictions out of self-pity.

Raising Expectations

Nancy's parents had low expectations for her, and she grew up with harsh punishments. She developed the habit of never expecting good things for herself so that she would not be disappointed. By age 40 she was grossly overweight, which ensured that many people would in fact reject her. When she was invited to a party, she wouldn't go because she thought the invitation came out of a sense of obligation, not because she was liked. She managed to be successful in a highly competitive business yet did not give herself credit for her success. She lived in pain and loneliness.

When she turned forty, she decided that it was time to change. She sought a mentor and found an older man who not only helped her to improve her business skills but also focused on her good qualities: her inner strength, her sense of humor, and her loving nature. Nancy followed his advice. She lost the weight and became comfortable with her body—and bought new clothes to show off her confidence. She made enough money to retire early and pursue her interests in art and self-improvement.

How We Induce Others to Be
What We Want Them to Be

We interpret our experience by making distinctions (is this good or bad, is it real or not real, is it here or there) and according to rules (never hurt others, avoid pain, don't intrude, punish yourself, and so on). In order to comply with these rules, we perform operations, wittingly or unwittingly, on our experience and on the experience of others. These are some of the operations.

DENIAL: Operating on our own experience: "I feel jealous" is changed to "I do not feel jealous." Mary had divorced her first husband when she discovered his infidelity. Now she was happily married to John, who worked in an office with several attractive women. From time to time Mary felt jealous, and she interrogated John about his activities at work. When John pointed out that there was no reason for her to be jealous, she indignantly replied, "I do not feel jealous." Because of her experience in her first marriage, jealousy was too painful an experience for her to admit to.

On another's experience: Jane said, "I am jealous." Lance replied, "You are not jealous." When Jane complained that she was jealous of Lance's relationship with his business partner, Lance told her, "You are not jealous—you are just trying to destroy my business."

DISPLACEMENT: On our own experience: "I feel angry at my wife instead of at my mother." Jim's mother was frequently critical of him. But Jim loved her dearly, so instead of responding to his mother's criticisms, it was easier for him to feel angry at his wife and pick a fight with her.

Sometimes Jim was actually upset at something that his wife had done, but invariably she would say, "You are not angry at me—you are angry at your mother."

SCOTOMATIZATION: I do not see what I do not want to see: Robert was very close to Cindy, his business partner, and often went on trips with her. Sometimes, Michele, his wife, suspected that they were having an affair, but she preferred not to think about it.

You do not see what I don't want you to see: One day Michele said to Robert, "When I went into your office, I saw that you had your arms around Cindy." Robert insisted, "You didn't see that because I didn't do that."

REPLACEMENT: I see something else instead: When Michele saw

Robert with his arm around Cindy, she thought that he was reaching for a book on the shelf.

You see something else instead: When Michele said that she saw Robert with his arm around Cindy, he said: "I was reaching for a book on the shelf."

PROJECTION: When I'm angry, I say that you are angry: Frank became angry every time his wife, Susan, asked him to do something around the house, so he responded by saying, "Why are you always so angry?"

When you say that I'm angry, I tell you that you are the angry one: Susan responded by saying, "You are the one who is angry."

INTROJECTION: When you are sad, I become sad: Tony couldn't stand seeing his wife, Amy, sad and would become sad himself.

I want you to be sad when I am sad: When Amy was sad, she wanted Tony to be sad with her.

RATIONALIZATION: I give myself a cover story: When Ruth was argumentative with her husband, she said it was because she was tired and stressed out from her job.

I give you a cover story: When Ruth was sarcastic, her husband would say, "You must have had a hard time at work."

REPRESSION: Forgetting something on purpose—and then forgetting that you have done so: James insulted his wife, Sandy, in front of her sister, Miriam. Some months later, Miriam mentioned the episode to Sandy, and Sandy said, "I don't remember that situation at all."

I want you to forget and forget that you have forgotten: Sandy said to James, "Could I have forgotten that you insulted me in front of Miriam?" James answered, "It never happened."

REGRESSION: I go back to the way I was in the past: When Chris has a cold, I treat him the way his mother did when he was sick as a child.

I want you to go back to the way you were in the past: Chris wanted his teenage children to admire him as they had when they were much younger.

IDENTIFICATION: I am just like you: When Jane complained to her mother about her shyness, the mother would say, "I'm as shy as you are."

You are just like me: Jane's mother used to say, "You are just like me; you will never be good at math."

MYSTIFICATION: This must not be what I think it is: When Clare found a love letter that David had written to another woman, she thought it was part of a story that he was writing.

This is not what you think it is: When David told Clare that he no longer loved her, she said, "This is just a passing mood."

REVERSAL: "I hate you" is reversed to "he hates me": Rose disliked her father-in-law and thought that he hated her.

When you say you hate him, I say he hates you: When Rose told her husband, Peter, that she hated his father, Peter said, "You've got it wrong. He is the one that hates you."

SPLITTING: I have two personalities—the good one and the bad one: Jill said, "I can't help it when I'm nasty. Sometimes another side of me comes out."

You have two personalities—the good one and the bad one: When Jill was angry, her husband said, "I'd better get out of the house. Your nasty personality is coming out."

PART II

BREAKING THROUGH TO THE RELATIONSHIP YOU WANT

Chapter 6

BE ALL OF WHO YOU REALLY ARE

Before we can truly change our relationships, we must first look deeply at ourselves—what beliefs we cling to, what decisions we may have made long ago that may be at the root of our relationship problem or that are preventing us from experiencing our full range of emotion. By identifying and changing patterns of belief and behavior that bring pain not only to us but also to others, we can transform ourselves and our relationships.

Let's look at how Anthony Robbins was able to help one woman reclaim her true identity, and by doing so also help her son and reconnect with her sister. I have outlined below the seven steps Tony used to help Lisa, which I will expand upon later in the chapter.

Steps to Reclaim Your True Identity

At a large international leadership conference, Lisa raised her hand with a simple question about her husband. Lisa was a 68-year-old Norwegian woman, who could easily be mistaken for a man—her short-cropped gray hair, the strength reflected in the deep lines of her face, and the way she held her muscular body all were at odds with her femininity.

Robbins quickly perceived that at the root of her problem was a decision she made as a child—one that had informed her entire adult life and crushed her intimate relationships.[1]

1. Challenge Limiting Beliefs and Identity

"When my husband gets angry," said Lisa, "I automatically get angry also, and then it feels like it is a matter of life and death."

"What does your husband do?" asked Tony.

"He becomes confused."

Tony immediately homed in on what he believed was the underlying issue: "He's used to dealing with you as if you were another man. He doesn't know how to deal with you being vulnerable. But vulnerability is power. It's not weakness. When you are vulnerable and allow yourself to feel emotions, you're connected to what's really true." In these few seconds, he had already identified Lisa's central guiding precept: never to be vulnerable.

Because in our culture vulnerability is associated with femininity, in refusing to ever appear vulnerable, Lisa had given up many of the pleasures of being a woman. Every person, to have balanced relationships, must be able to sometimes be vulnerable and sometimes be strong. Robbins guessed that Lisa gave up the possibility of being vulnerable when she was a child, and only now had begun to experience moments of vulnerability—and it felt terrifying to her. Robbins needed to discover the root cause of her loss of femininity and vulnerability in order to help her.

He made contact with her from across the room, smiling broadly, opening his arms, and teasing her with questions like how often she danced naked around her house. Then he asked the crucial question: "Tell me about your father."

Lisa explained that her father was a huge, fat man who was very strict and beat her when she misbehaved.

"When he hit you, how did you cope with it?" asked Robbins.

"I didn't laugh, of course, but I couldn't care less," said Lisa with a certain pride.

"That's right. You got harder, didn't you?" said Tony looking at her intently, "and tougher. So you became a man to try to survive. What would have happened if you had cried and gone crazy? What would he have done?"

"I have a guess because my sister cried and he stopped."

"That's right," Robbins said softly and paused, giving time for Lisa to think.

She hesitated. "I thought it was humiliating."

"I know . . . I know."[2]

2. Discover and Understand the Key Decision

Lisa's head went back, her eyes fixed on the ceiling in a pained gesture of astonishment. In that very second she realized how her childhood, her entire life could have been different. Sixty years ago she had made a decision about how to respond to her abusive father. Only now did she suddenly understand that there had been a choice—and that she had made one. She had wanted her father's love so much. She had been beaten while her sister got away with anything. As she talked to Robbins, that fear of weakness, of dependence came over her again.

"But I didn't want him to win," she said.

"I know, honey." Robbins wanted to reassure Lisa that her feelings were okay.

"It wasn't very nice."

"It was horrible. It was abusive. It was wrong. If he was here, I would let him know in a way that he would not forget." There was anger in Robbins's voice.

"I loved him."

"I know. You still do. So you became like him. You tried to become his son in order to get his love."

Every woman in the room knew that she either was like Lisa, or was closely connected to someone like Lisa. Every man knew someone like Lisa's father, or dreaded to think that he actually might be like Lisa's father.

3. Connect to the Consequences of the Key Decision

Robbins helped Lisa to realize the negative repercussions that her key decision had on her most significant relationships. He asked her about her children and discovered that her son, Ralph, had been weak and dependent on his wife, who had recently left him. As Lisa talked with Robbins about her son, she suddenly realized that Ralph had tried to turn his wife into someone like his mother and that was part of the failure of the marriage. This was the opportunity for Robbins to get Lisa to commit to change.

4. Commit to Changing

"What are we going to do?" he asked her. "Are we responsible to do something about this since we have this awareness and understanding, or should we just gloss over it and say, 'There's nothing that can be done.'"

"No," said Lisa firmly. "That's one thing I really want to do something about."

"You have to sit down with your son," said Robbins, "and tell him that you've been living your life as a man, and as a result he developed a great sensitivity to responding to you as a man, and that is beautiful. But you have done him wrong without meaning to, because you made him think that feminine is weak and ugly because you are his idea of a woman. Tell him he's never known you, never known the real you, because you have been covering that up your whole life. And then ask him to take you shopping."

Lisa laughed at the absurdity of asking her son to take her shopping, yet she clearly understood that this would be a totally out-of-character behavior that would impress her son. Robbins had asked Lisa to apologize to her son as her first step in becoming feminine. He knew he had to direct her to specific actions that would reverse some of the consequences of her key decision.

5. Build Up Emotional Resources

Then he discovered the source of greatest pain: the sister whom Lisa had resented and rejected because she was vulnerable and had been spared the father's violence.

"What about your sister?" asked Robbins.

"I almost said, 'She's a bitch,' but that would be inappropriate," said Lisa.

"I see the anger you have for her because you thought she stole love from you. And you hated her for it your whole life, and you've tried to not be like her your whole life, and you've judged her your whole life."

"I have. And I have six grandchildren. If they get involved in this thing also. . . ."

Robbins laughed, delighted that Lisa wanted to change for the sake of her grandchildren. "I want you to talk to your sister," he said, "and tell her how sorry you are that you've hated her all these years, when all she wanted was love, just like you. And I don't care if she treats you badly. I don't want you to do it for her. I want you to do it for your son and your grandchildren."

"I wanted so much to love her."

"Where do you feel the love?" asked Robbins.

Lisa pointed to her heart.

"Feel your breast gently," said Robbins. "Think about your sister. She's hurting. And now you can feel what she really feels. Before, you thought she was just a bitch. Now, you feel that she's hurting, because when you're feminine you can feel everything. No one has to tell you. And you know things no one could possibly know. You know them in here, don't you? What does she need?"

"She needs love."

"Whose love does she need right now?"

"I think she needs mine, and she needs my acceptance."

"Yes. Who needs her love and acceptance?"

"I need her."

6. Strategize Ways to Reclaim Your Identity

"When would be a good time to make that happen?"

"For instance, now," said Lisa.

"Can you feel her acceptance right now?"

"Yes, yes, yes, I can feel it."

"I want you to feel all her love for you in your body right now, the love she's had for you since a little girl, the love she's had for you even when she was mean or you were mean. Feel it to the point that it's overwhelming." Lisa closed her eyes as Robbins continued. "And she's really a girl, isn't she? She's the girl you've been trying not to be like your whole life. But you're her sister, and you are like her. You always have been."

"I suddenly see that I admired her because of the way she dressed. She was tall and slim and a dancer."

"And she got a lot of attention for that, attention you weren't getting. So even though you loved and admired her, you learned not to value those things. You learned to reject those things, and you learned to reject her, even though you really love her. What would your sister call you if she were to give you a nickname?"

"Liz. She even named her daughter Liz."

The audience applauded. This was the confirmation of how much Lisa's sister loved her, but Lisa just looked puzzled. "I thought she stole my name," she said.

"And she is one of the only people in your whole life who loved you unconditionally. Not even your father loved you unconditionally."

"No, he didn't," said Lisa. "She's one of the only ones ever. It's unbelievably true. It's true."

"Except she stole your name for her daughter," said Robbins. "What a thief!" The audience laughed, amazed at how Lisa could have had that idea.

7. Take Specific Action and Visualize the Benefits

Robbins ended the intervention by projecting Lisa into the future through a visualization that began by focusing her on the present, then leading her to the future, where she would experience all the good and the happiness that would result from her transformation. Now Lisa could experience the strength of vulnerability and, with this newfound strength, return to her family to guide them with enlightenment and wisdom.

Robbins saw Lisa again 8 months later. She reported many amazing changes. She had spoken with her son as soon as she got back to Norway. A few weeks later, he fell in love with a wonderful woman with whom he was very happy. With a twinkle in her eye, Lisa explained that she now goes shopping with girlfriends and enjoys it.

But the best of all is her relationship with her sister. "I am an artist," said Lisa, "and recently I had an art show, so I invited my sister to the opening. She came and we were talking to a common friend. The friend asked my sister, 'How do you know you are loved?' And my sister answered, 'When my sister, Lisa, invites me to her art show, I know that she loves me.'"

Lisa was tearful as she talked about this. "I started crying," she continued. "It was so little, in a way. In the past my sister always said, 'Nobody loves me.' It mattered so much to her, and I was filled with love for her, not pity, just love, and that was fantastic. It's absolutely amazing with my sister. It has made an enormous impact on her that I have changed. I don't know what I do that's different, but in the past she was always whining, and she had all these pains and wanted everybody to feel sorry for her. Now she calls me and talks to me normally, no pains, no complaints. She wants me to help her with her relationship with her youngest daughter. It's so fantastic because I have all these ideas about how we could change. My sister could take the role of being grandmother in my family, and I could be grandmother in her family!"

Change Is Always Possible

Most of what we call our "identity" comes from choices we make: what we choose to focus on, what skills we develop, how we relate to others, how we want others to see us. However, we tend to forget that the source of our identity is actually a result of these choices, past and present. We become what we think is expected of us and assume it is just a part of who we are. It can be very difficult to see ourselves differently and make real changes to our identity.

Is it possible to change a key decision that has shaped us, even if it's been a part of us for 20 years or longer? Of course, it is. We have all seen it happen. People quit smoking after 20 years, become athletes after a sedentary life, marry for love instead of security, learn to trust and communicate after a life of isolation. It is after people rediscover and bring to light the reason why they made a key decision in the past—what needs they were meeting and what the benefits and consequences of that decision were—that they are able to make a new decision that will allow them to experience the fullness of their lives and their relationships.

"True identity" does not mean any one of the facets of our identity (mother, wife, executive, or athlete). It encompasses our model of the world—how we learned to satisfy or even to suppress our most important needs. How we built our model of the world. All of our lives, we have been making decisions that verge on the superhuman: We decided it was time to learn to walk; we decided to learn to read; we decided to become independent from our parents. With each of these decisions, we let go of who we thought we were and rose to another level of being. That's what we mean by true identity—your ability, at the deepest level, to make the decisions that will allow you to achieve a new level of fulfillment and to let go of the beliefs and behaviors that hold you back. You can use the same steps Tony used with Lisa to reclaim your true identity.

Step One: Challenge Limiting Beliefs and Identity

Who says a man can't be vulnerable or sensitive? Who says a man can't cry? Who says a career woman with a family can't also be fun loving and carefree? A sensitive man can be strong. A woman can be sexy and feminine and stay in control. The fears that caused us to limit our full range of feelings might have been useful in the past, but may well be obsolete and wreaking havoc in our important relationships.

Challenging yourself doesn't mean that you should beat yourself up, feel guilty, or think of yourself as "wrong." Instead, you need to separate aspects of your behavior that no longer serve the true essence of who you are. Sometimes, in order to solve a problem, we need to create a new image of who we think we are. We need to make a new decision, to try something that pushes us out of the identity that is known, safe, and comfortable for us, but that may be limiting our ability to feel joy, passion, love, and connection.

Go back in time to a key decision you made, and this time choose the path you didn't choose before. Focus on the parts of yourself and the feelings that you have neglected, the parts you've spent your life trying to overcome. Perhaps, like Lisa, you fear being vulnerable; perhaps, like her son, you fear being strong. Or you may have decided you cannot truly trust anyone, or that you will never be pretty enough, intelligent enough, or thin enough. Remember when you first made your key decision or adopted your belief. Remember what your life was like then, and why you made that decision then. Today you can make a different decision to bring greater range and balance to your life.

Consider the different areas of your life and your relationships. What do you spend the most time focusing on? What gives you the most satisfaction? Where do you feel unfulfilled? Is there something that is particularly frustrating?

Step Two: Discover and Understand the Key Decision

Go back to your childhood. Ask yourself: What kind of person was your father? Your mother? How did they treat you? What other significant people influenced you? What experiences had a profound impact on you and helped determine who you became? When did you make your key decision—whether it was not to trust, not to show vulnerability, not to show your strength, not to forgive? You can probably remember the precise moment when you made that decision.

What Has Been Painful for You?

Key decisions are usually made during moments of crisis. If you take yourself back to a powerful key experience—of fear, pain, hurt, or humiliation—whether in your childhood or adulthood, you will discover needs, feelings, fears, and emotions that you hadn't recognized or articulated at the time.

What Other Options Did You Have?

We have all been through difficult experiences, some of which were almost impossible to bear. However, we rarely recognize that, in those moments, we made a key decision. We decided to act, not act, or react in a certain way. These are the decisions that have the most powerful influence over how we conduct our lives. Perhaps it is because they are so powerful that we rarely recognize them as decisions. Key decisions are often made amidst such challenging circumstances that most people come to assume that the way they chose to act was their only possible choice.

How Did the Key Decision Serve You?

If you are like most people, when you think of the difficult times in your life, you will think of them as events that happened to you. It is rare for an individual to look back on her life and see it through the prism of her own decisions. It is even more unusual to look back on those decisions and recognize how they served you at the time. Here is a useful rule of thumb: Any time you repeat a behavior—be it anger, depression, helplessness, or fortitude—it is because you are gaining something from it. It may be difficult to really examine what you're getting from such behavior, but it is a critical step in developing your true capacity.

Lisa was able to see that she decided never to show hurt or vulnerability in order to deal with her father's abuse. She thought that made her a "winner" rather than a victim. In fact, it led her to deny the feminine, vulnerable, emotional part of herself.

Reflect now on a difficult moment in your own life. How did you react? Who else was there, and how did they react? What kind of decision did you make? Did you decide to be strong and face the challenge, or did you take a position of vulnerability? What were you feeling? Did you decide to trust others, or did you decide to rely on yourself? Did you put your faith in a set of beliefs or values? Did you focus on your feelings, on other people's behavior, on external circumstances, or did you just want to run away? You may not have thought this out at the time, but at the moment you responded to that difficulty, a powerful decision was made. What did you decide? State it simply: That is a Key Decision.

Step Three: Connect to the Consequences of the Key Decision

You may have decided never to trust anyone, and now you can't trust your husband. Perhaps because you had difficult parents, you focus on work—you decided it was better to focus on numbers and objects rather than on people. Consider one-by-one the consequences that the key decision had in your relationships with your spouse, children, family, and friends.

Every decision carries consequences beyond the immediate situation. It affects not only other decisions you make in the future but also the people with whom you interact.

Most key decisions control one or more areas of your life. Is it marriage, your family life, your romantic relationships, your work relationships, or your financial habits? Who else has been affected or influenced by that decision? How? Did your key decision have negative consequences for others?

Step Four: Commit to Changing

Tell yourself "enough is enough," and realize that an obsolete decision no longer needs to keep you from loving and living to your fullest. You'll be surprised how powerful it is to say it out loud, over and over. It's also powerful to write it down, and post it somewhere you'll see it often.

The environment in which you grew up influenced your decisions and may have prompted you to devise certain strategies to protect yourself. Your family or environment today is probably very different. You may have made a key decision recently—perhaps to protect yourself from your husband's criticism or teasing, or to make sure that you were the one to decide how to invest your inheritance—that may become a problem for your spouse or your children in the future. If you can identify ways that your key decision may directly lead to negative outcomes for you or for those you care about, it's time to make an adjustment.

Make that change now. It may not be drastic; perhaps only a small adjustment is necessary.

Step Five: Build Up Emotional Resources

Do one small thing that contradicts the key decision from the past. For example, if you've always been afraid to show your wife your most vulnerable, tender feelings, let her see them now. If you always react with anger or stoicism to your husband's teasing, this time allow yourself to show your hurt: Cry in front of him. If you feel you have to repress your exuberance because your child is sad, do something fun or outrageous with him.

It is also important to emphasize the ways in which you have succeeded in life. If you begin to feel overwhelmed with regret or guilt, put things into perspective. The purpose of this seven-step process is to enhance your ability to make the best possible decisions *today.* In order to do this, you must take full responsibility for the past decisions you have made and the ways they have affected you and others. But keep in mind as you do this that it's not useful to dwell on feelings of guilt and regret for past actions and other things that lie outside your control. Also, it is important to remember that no matter how deeply others have been influenced by you, they are responsible for their own key decisions as well. Take responsibility for your choices, and support others in taking responsibility for theirs.

Take a moment to recognize and appreciate the way that your key decision has served you—and your significant others. Perhaps your decision to focus on work over family life has led you to become a great business success and be well-off financially. Perhaps your focus on your strength rather than your vulnerability has shown your children how they, too, can survive and rise to any challenge. These skills and achievements are yours to keep. Observe the ways those around you have been stimulated and helped by your key decision.

Every decision involves excluding possibilities. When you made your key decision, what other alternatives did you give up? What adjustments could you make to your key decision that would allow you not only to maintain the benefits but also to experience the things that you have sacrificed? Who else might benefit if you made this adjustment and reclaimed some of those resources?

Step Six: Strategize Ways to Reclaim Your Identity

Make a plan. Like Lisa, you may want to visit your siblings and talk about how vulnerable you felt in the family. A man who decided it was dangerous to express his feelings openly might try to be openly affectionate to his wife in front of his male colleagues. A wife may decide to act strong and decisive. A husband may decide to share his sadness and fear. Surprise your loved ones by expressing feelings that you have been keeping to yourself.

Apologize for the Way
Your Key Decision Has Hurt Others

It is important in this process to acknowledge that others have been affected by our key decisions and, when possible, to directly apologize to them. Following are three steps for making an apology.

1. **Appreciate.** Express appreciation and admiration for the way others have grown and developed in relation to you and your key decision.

2. **Set context.** Apologize for not living up to your own potential and for the extent that others were negatively affected by your actions. Demonstrate your willingness and ability to change.

3. **Express regret for direct harm.** If you find that a key decision you have made has led to serious, direct harm to another, it is important that you show sincere regret, a determination never to do it again, and a desire to amend for your actions. However, you do not need to ask for forgiveness—your apology should require nothing from anyone else.

Reclaim Long-Lost Possibilities

Now it is time to strategize how to bring new experiences and ways of being in your life and relationships. Think of many wonderful things that you can do, now that you have recovered your true identity.

Use Your Physiology to Find Your Emotion

When you want to experience your full emotional range, it is important to use all of the resources at your disposal, including your physiology. Ask yourself what you could do physically to find your emotion. If you have been protecting your vulnerability, maybe you need to focus on feeling your heart. If you have been afraid to show fear, perhaps you need to focus on standing up straight, pulling your shoulders back, and feeling powerful. If you've been afraid to express exuberance or joy, perhaps you need (in private) to wave your arms in the air and jump up and down.

Step Seven: Take Specific Action and Visualize the Benefits

Decide when, where, and how—and imagine the reactions of your partner, friends, and relatives. Then do it!

Once you have discovered what new decisions and feelings you want to experience, make an absolute commitment to action. Think of how your new key decision will improve all your relationships. Say and do things that you have never done before so that your new identity will be firmly established.

Use the seven steps described in this chapter any time you feel yourself shying away from something you want to do or are capable of doing. You may go through all of the steps each time, or you may find that some steps resonate more powerfully with you than others. Once you go through the steps several times, they will become second nature. The next time you start feeling overwhelmed, ask yourself:

What decision am I dealing with here?

When did I make it?

Why did I make it?

What does it accomplish?

What are its side effects?

What decision can I make now?

Chapter 7

THE SEVEN MASTER STEPS OF RELATIONSHIP BREAKTHROUGH

There are seven master steps that you can use to break through to the relationship you want. Once you master this process, it can be applied not only to your relationships but also to other aspects of your life.

These steps were developed by Anthony Robbins and informed by the pioneering work of Milton Erickson. Obviously, some of these steps, such as "understanding," are essential to all human interaction, but Erickson contributed the most subtle understanding of metaphors, beliefs, language, and values. As important was his elucidation of subtle ways to break patterns in relationships and create new, unexpected possibilities.[1]

Step One: Understand Your Model of the World and the Other Person's Model of the World

As we now know, the first step in resolving a conflict is to change our focus from the immediate conflict to the underlying unsolved needs that are causing the conflict. Whenever you are trying to bring change in a relationship, you must first understand what needs you and the other person value most, how each of you habitually meets those needs, and what is preventing those needs from being met. To influence another person (or to change yourself), you must understand their model of the world—their core beliefs and values, the emotions they habitually experience—as well as the other people and decisions that influence them. You can't change someone without knowing what already influences them. You have to dig and be proactive. Notice— when you push, how does the other person react? When you are pushed, how do you react? Do you call your mother? Do you bury yourself in work? Do you turn to drugs, alcohol, or food?

With empathy and understanding comes appreciation for the circumstances and challenges both you and the other person bring to the relationship. Empathy is essential for change.

Understanding can occur at three levels:

1. The Individual

    What needs you (or the other) value most

    What vehicles you (or the other) use for meeting your needs

    What is your (or the other's) model of the world

    What brings you (or the other) pain

2. The Relationship

    What needs are being met in your relationship

    How are these needs being met

    What are the rules of the relationship

    What weapons are habitually being used

3. The System

    Who communicates with whom and how

    Who has power over whom and in what way

    What is the hierarchy

Let's look more at Paul and Jenn, our couple from Chapters 2 through 5, as they continued to work with Tony Robbins. Jenn's two most important needs were certainty and love. For Jenn's love to be able to flow freely, she had to feel certain first. She, however, was going through a time of great uncertainty, both financially and emotionally. Because Jenn felt most certain about her family and children, she turned to them to satisfy her need for love rather than turning to Paul.

Many people who live in uncertain times can still allow their love to flow freely. Tony pointed out to Jenn that if she changed her first need to love instead of certainty, she would change her relationship with Paul.

For Paul the most important needs were love and significance. He felt insignificant because he was not providing for Jenn and his family in the way she wanted. He felt he came fifth or sixth after the children and her family in terms of her love. Paul turned to his work to find significance and to his mother and sisters to find love. Paul used his threat of leaving the marriage as a weapon against Jenn, and Jenn's teasing and sarcasm were her weapons against Paul.

I have created a series of exercises in the workbook section that will take you step-by-step through the process of truly discovering not only your own needs, model of the world, vehicles, emotions, and influences but your partner's as well. Once you truly understand one another, change can be created based on your understanding of each other, your relationship, and the larger system of your interaction. At an individual level, if you understand that you are driven by significance, for instance, you might find new and better ways to meet that need. Similarly, you may want to help your partner to find better ways to meet his or her need for significance. You need to elicit the story that he has been telling himself—what has his life been about? What has yours? What character are you playing? What is the genre of your story? In the workbook, you will find specific exercises to help you do this.

Let's say that you understand that your business partner is driven by the need for certainty, so you make every effort to provide that certainty. If you are trying to help your daughter with her marriage and you understand that her husband is driven by the need to make a contribution, you help her to find ways to encourage and help him in fulfilling that need. If you understand that you and your husband are not fulfilling each other's most important needs, you find ways to make this a top priority, helping him to understand what you need and ensuring that you fulfill his needs. For almost any relationship to be successful in the long run, the need for love and connection must come first. If, like Jenn, another unmet need is preventing focus on love and connection, how can you change that?

At the systems level, you need to understand how you communicate, what weapons you or your partner habitually uses, who has power in the relationship, who is in a higher position in the hierarchy, who else is involved in the relationship, and if that involvement creates a triangle or is part of a circle. It is important to understand whether or not those who appear to be powerful are truly so. Sometimes the weak are powerful, and the powerful are weak. There may also be hierarchical incongruities in your relationship that need to be made explicit and looked at carefully.

Before we can make major changes, we must first understand our primary needs, our emotions, and our model of the world.

Step Two: Get Leverage

All of us can change, but we must truly want to, and be willing to do what's necessary to break through our habitual patterns and find a new way of acting. We must discover our own emotional resources, those of our partner, and those of our relationships. Then we need to commit to making the changes that will solve the problem.

Once you have completed the exercises in the workbook, you will see the problem in a new way and discover the resources that can lead to positive change. Now that you know what both you and your partner really need, challenge the rules and the vehicles by which you have been meeting those needs. Find the old challenges. Determine what already influences you and your partner.

Raising the Level of Pain

People want to change when they experience discomfort in the way they are meeting their needs. When this discomfort is not strong enough to motivate someone to change, you can gain leverage by raising the level of pain that is caused by meeting needs in unsatisfactory ways. Project the person into the future. Ask: If you don't change, what will it mean? Who will it hurt? What will it cost you? Discuss what the consequences will be in the future if change doesn't happen now. You can even create a punishment for not changing. (For example, Milton Erickson encouraged a man with insomnia to get out of bed and scrub the floors for an hour when he couldn't sleep. Then he was to get back in bed and, if he wasn't asleep in 15 minutes, to get up and scrub the floors again, and to do this all night. The insomnia disappeared.) When the pain is sufficient, you will discover the possibility of change. Change occurs when there is immediate pain for not changing now and immediate pleasure for changing now. Leverage is most effective when it is immediate.

Tony got leverage with Paul by pointing out all that he would lose in a divorce: His children would hate him at times; another man would probably raise them; and he would lose much more money than he anticipated. Tony pointed out to Jenn that by hanging on to her need for certainty, she was losing her femininity and not letting her love flow. He also told her that her sarcasm could make it difficult to love her.

Leverage means to get maximum access or use out of your resources. You can leverage yourself in a relationship by understanding what matters most to you. What do you want from the relationship? Take a moment to daydream. What would bring you pleasure, satisfaction, and fulfillment? What kind of effort are you ready to undertake in order to realize your vision? How will your partner feel, knowing that you are doing everything in your power to love and serve him or her? What will the consequences be if you do not make this commitment to your partner?

When we are ready to change, we will, of course, want to use all the tools we have to evaluate our own needs, our model of the world, the shape of our extended relationships, and our ways of communicating. We can also call on a powerful tool of self-analysis that can add another dimension in helping us to reframe a problem.

Using Archetypes

Archetypes are characters that appear universally in myths and are contained within each of us. There are four universal Jungian archetypes.

The Warrior. The Warrior is action and strength. This is the strongest, most intense part of us. The Warrior is powerful and focused on action. The Warrior attacks a problem. This archetype can engage your full emotional commitment to solving a problem so that you are fully vested before moving on. Alternative names for the Warrior are the Fighter, the Soldier, the Protector, the Amazon, and the Hero.

The Magician. The Magician is humor and imagination. The Magician signifies imagination, intuition, and humor. Once you have fully engaged as the Warrior, moving to the archetype of the Magician encourages you to break patterns, even the pattern of being a Warrior. The Magician is irreverent and uses humor as a shortcut. The Magician tells the untold truth about the situation and in that way finds options for the solution. The Magician can detach from anything and just observe it. He finds the magic in everything. The Magician can snap his fingers and change things. What other people get upset about, he sees as absurd because he has a totally different perspective. The Magician sees that it's all magic, it's all hocus pocus, it's all spells. He has a bit of a whimsical view of things, and he is involved with the invisible and with intuition. He can solve things in an instant. Whereas the Warrior has to do things through strength, power, and action, the Magician might do it with the snap of a finger, by insight, or by humor. Alternative names for the Magician are the Maverick, the Wise Guy, the Fairy Godmother, the Turnaround Expert.

The Lover. The Lover is deep connection. The Lover signifies your deepest emotional connection with others and with the world. The love that sustained you in your childhood is the basis of your feeling of conscience and compassion for others. This is where you vibrate with life and connect to yourself and to other people. This is where your deepest love is—a love that has no conditions, a love that is pure, the purest part of who you are. Alternative names for the Lover are the Caretaker, the Protector, the Loving One.

The Sovereign. The Sovereign is vision and purpose. The Sovereign integrates the other archetypes into a comprehensive vision about your life and purpose. He or she is the one who really knows your vision and objectives. The Sovereign is the one who governs and has the ability to rule your life. He knows why you are here, what you are here to do. The Sovereign is like a great king or queen with enormous wisdom and knowledge. He has been here before; he commands and never overreacts. Alternative names for the Sovereign are the King or Queen, the Visionary, the Founder, the Goddess, the President.

These archetypes are in each of us, but they are not always in balance. Sometimes the Warrior is running the show, and every action comes from that perspective. Sometimes it is the Lover, whose actions are quite different. But whenever only one is in charge, that perspective becomes exhausted.

Play out your problem in the persona of each of these archetypes. What does the Warrior want? What does the Lover want? And so on. This is a way of creating your own network—a circle of support to help you get to the root of what is wrong. I will go into greater depth with this technique in Chapter 9. This process harnesses the force of emotion, turning it into a strength that will bring about harmony.

Leverage can be obtained by calling on your archetypes or calling on others for support and help. It can also be achieved by raising the level of pain. A person can be motivated to change if not changing will bring pain or the fear of pain to herself or to others. A person can also be motivated to change through the compassion and support of others. In the examples at the end of this chapter, you will see several ways leverage can be used.

Conflict with our loved one is a great motivator for change—we would rather change than lose a relationship. The intervention of someone we respect—a friend, parent, or counselor—can also be a strong motivator for change.

Step Three: Interrupt Limiting/Destructive Habitual Patterns

As we have seen, most of us follow a core emotional pattern that dictates what we do to satisfy our needs.

Physiology, focus, and meaning are the triad that determines our habitual patterns. In order to bring about change, you must interrupt these patterns. For example, "depression" consists of a certain physiological state, a focus on certain events and thoughts, and the meaning that is given to those events and thoughts. However, if at the moment when you are "depressed," someone can make you laugh, the pattern has been interrupted. The momentary experience of laughter can be expanded upon, demonstrating that "depression" is always under your control and that it can shift instantaneously to laughter. You can interrupt a pattern by asking an outrageous question, using shocking language, telling a joke, or scaring the person with a loud noise or a threatening move. Such a move will actually change their breathing pattern, thus changing their physiology.

All of us have habitual patterns that can be damaging to a loving relationship. What do we do to interrupt those patterns and prevent them from sabotaging our relationships? The first step is to be able to listen to your partner. When you express your true feelings to each other, one or the other of you may feel sensitive or hurt. This is a sign of closeness. As you listen to your partner, be prepared to hear some things that may sound like complaints, criticisms, or accusations. You will have a choice as to whether you will hear these statements as criticism of you or as requests of you to meet your partner's needs. Remember that such requests indicate caring at a deep level—they signify that your partner believes you can provide what she needs. Discover together how to satisfy your partner, thereby satisfying both of you.

It may be as simple as doing one small thing differently. When you change the where, the when, the how, or the with whom, the entire interaction changes. For example, set a special time and a special place to deliberately have a fight. A deliberate fight is not the same as a spontaneous one, and your habitual pattern would have been interrupted. Or your pattern may be that the wife always criticizes the husband and the husband defends himself. What happens if the husband makes one criticism of the wife, and the wife then criticizes his criticism? This will interrupt their habitual pattern. Don't be afraid to be physical or outrageous. Think back to the men in Chapter 1 who stopped their wives' nagging by taking off their clothes. What would happen if every time your husband complained about you, you began jumping up and down like a monkey?

At the systems level, it is usually a coalition of two-against-one that is creating the problem. For example, a husband may need to be blocked from siding with his mother against his wife, or a wife blocked from siding with her child against her husband.

Looking again at Paul and Jenn, Tony explicitly asked Paul to distance himself from his mother and sisters, and he asked Jenn to block her sources of certainty and love by making Paul more important than anyone else.

When habitual patterns are interrupted, new choices become available.

Step Four: Define the Problem in Solvable Terms

Whatever the challenge you are facing, you must define it in a way that it can be resolved. Often we trap ourselves because we define our challenge in unsolvable terms, so vague and abstract or so concrete and detailed that it cannot be resolved. The real challenge is always to find new ways of meeting our human needs. Again, what prevents us from doing so is our habitual pattern of emotions and physiology (the state of the body—the energy level), what we focus on, and the meaning we give to events.

There are many different ways of understanding and defining what we want to change. Ultimately, our success will depend upon how we have understood and formulated the issue to be resolved. For example, "depression" is difficult to resolve, but "boredom" is simple to take care of. "Impulse control" is a challenge, but "a bad temper" is easy. It's hard to resolve "incompatibility," but it's easy to improve "communication." "Personality clashes" are difficult, but "negotiating different points of view" is easier.

Sometimes a more extreme definition of the problem is actually easier to resolve. I recently helped a couple with four very young children. The wife, who was 35 years old, had recklessly had an affair with a 22-year-old. The husband was outraged, deeply hurt, and ready to leave her. She wanted to save the marriage and didn't know how to justify her behavior. I explained to them that she probably had been suffering from "temporary insanity." She had been temporarily insane, and the husband, instead of outrage, should feel compassion, take care of her, and restore her sanity. Her brother had died in an accident the year before, and I attributed her insanity to her grieving process. The husband knew what to do about an unfaithful wife but didn't have a clue as to what to do about insanity; therefore, he had to follow my advice. The alleged "insanity" elicited his sympathy. They stayed together, and today they are very happy.

Instead of focusing on Jenn's looks, on attraction, or on compatibility, Tony focused on how Paul and Jenn could satisfy each other's needs. This was a problem that was easy to solve. Jenn's dad used to call her "Sweetie." Paul discovered that he only had to call Jenn "Sweetie" to bring out all her affection. Small things make a big difference. Using a term of endearment he knew she liked allowed her to drop her defenses and to respond warmly.

The way you define a problem is crucial as to whether you will be able to solve it.

Step Five: Create New Empowering Alternatives

Once you have interrupted habitual patterns, you must create empowering alternatives. Within our imagination, we can find unlimited alternatives that can be used to create new physiological states, a different focus, new questions and beliefs. You must find all the options that are available, creating multiple ways to meet the most important needs. Find new alternatives in your own language, beliefs, focus, decisions, as well as in communication and relationships with others. Make plans, assign yourself tasks, and think about your key decisions, how you define yourself, and how you approach others. Tell stories, use metaphors, try paradoxical solutions, and don't forget to use the power of humor. You will see all these in the examples at the end of the chapter.

Remember that we cannot eliminate a behavior or belief without replacing it with something that meets or exceeds the needs met by the previous behavior. Empower yourself and your loved one to think and act differently. Remember past moments of empowerment. Brainstorm ways to achieve that empowered feeling again, meeting needs at the same level or higher. Find empowering role models.

Think about your beliefs about yourself. What are your incantations—what do you say to yourself that prevents you from accomplishing what you want, from being who you want to be? We all have a voice inside our head that repeats the same old, tired phrases. What does your voice say? Is it: "I'm not smart enough," "I'm stupid," or "I'm not attractive"? Change those incantations to the positive: "I can do it," "I'm smart," or "I'm good looking." Get the bad incantations out of your head.

Most people have a primary question—the question that defines their identity. For some it may be "How can I best help others?" Or "How can I make this better?" For others, the question might be "How can I have more fun?" What is your primary question? Change it to one that empowers you and allows you to succeed. Here are some questions that you can ask to elicit your primary question: What would be an even more powerful way to meet your six human needs? Which emotions do you need to strengthen? What's the truth that can set you free?

For example, if a man thinks he must accomplish in order to feel loved, give him multiple ways in which he can feel loved, perhaps organizing his children to show him love or making sure he is appreciated at home and rewarded for things other than accomplishments.

At the end of their time with Tony, Paul and Jenn spontaneously created their own more empowering alternatives. When Tony asked them what they would promise each other, Jenn said that she would make Paul number one in her life. Paul said that he would show Jenn a strength and a love that she had never imagined him capable of.

Focus on a new, more positive way of meeting your needs.

Step Six: Condition the New Thought/ Emotion/Decision/Action

We need to ensure that the positive change will continue in the future by anticipating the obstacles, solutions, and rewards that lie ahead. Try to project yourself and your loved one into the future and anticipate obstacles that might arise—and the ways you might overcome them. Try to visualize all that's good from the past and project it into the future. Envision all the benefits that will occur in the future from having made the change. Anticipate all the pain and negativity that would result from not sustaining the change. Create specific negative consequences for not sustaining the change and devise rewards for sustaining the positive change.

Paul and Jenn conditioned their new resolve by making their promises to each other in the presence of Jenn's sister and brother-in-law and in the midst of the applause of the 2,000 people present at the event.

Conditioning yourself to be unselfish and devoted is quite difficult unless you back it up with actions that produce pleasure for you and the person who will receive your generosity.

Develop a ritual, a way of embodying your new standard in life and love.

Step Seven: Relate to a Higher Purpose or Connect to an Empowering Environment

When making any big change, or any significant new commitment, it is essential to relate that new commitment to a higher purpose, your highest hopes for your relationships, and the benefit for your life as a whole. When we take on a responsibility that requires effort or sacrifice, it is essential that we remind ourselves of the meaning and function of that new choice in our lives. Take a moment to ask yourself these questions: What is the greater purpose of bringing about this change? Who will benefit? If you have children, what will this do for them? What will this do for them as an example of how to live? How will it influence your children, your grandchildren, and great-grandchildren?

How will this change relate to what you value most and to what you ultimately want to accomplish? How does the change fulfill all six human needs in a sustainable way? What are you grateful for right this moment?

Paul and Jenn have devoted themselves to helping couples in their community, and they wrote a book about their relationship.

Focus on how to create an environment that will sustain the change.

Relationship Breakthroughs

These seven steps are the general principles behind all relationship break-throughs. While working our way through the seven steps, specific solutions are developed for specific challenges. Here are three examples of how the seven steps have been used in different situations.

Focusing on Father

Beth was the 15-year-old daughter of Walter, a famous Washington lawyer. She was referred to me by a prestigious university hospital, where she had been hospitalized many times for anorexia. She looked very ill and presented the typical thought disorder that one sees in these cases: She believed there was nothing wrong with her, in spite of several hospitalizations, and that her eating habits were perfectly healthy.

Father and daughter came to see me alone for the first session. Walter and Beth's mother, Joan, were divorced, and the mother was away on a trip with her charity, even though it was clear that the daughter's life was in danger. I got her on the phone, however, and she was present by our second meeting.

Walter and Joan had married 2 months after Walter's father died. Walter considered the marriage to be a reaction to his grief, and he and Joan divorced before Beth was born. They shared joint custody of Beth and lived a few blocks from each other.

Joan was the only child of Holocaust survivors. She had no living relatives, and an aunt had died of anorexia. Walter, a brilliant, powerful man, was remarried and had another child. Joan hated Walter, and Walter felt contempt for Joan.

Joan was emotionally frail, insecure, somewhat disorganized, and lonely. I realized that, in Beth's mind, she felt that she would never be able to leave home. She thought she would always have to take care of her mother because Joan had no one else. Beth also felt that she had to protect her mother from Walter's viciousness, a daunting task for a young girl. (*With these thoughts I had completed step one: Understanding Beth's world.*)

So I met alone with Walter. "You are very intelligent, so I'm going to be very frank and clear with you. I don't want to waste your time or mine. It's up to you to save your daughter's life, and you can decide whether you want to or not. In the endless war between you and your ex-wife, your daughter is taking all the bullets. For her sake, you can no longer have one harsh word, one unpleasant gesture toward Joan. Not only that, but you must go out of your way to help Joan and take care of her in every way you can, materially and emotionally. From now on, at least three times a day, I want you to tell Beth that you love her mother, not as a wife but as the mother of your child, and that you're always going to take care of her. And then you're going to do just that. Every day, you will call Joan and ask her if there is anything you can do to help her, and then you will do it."

(With this intervention I had used my leverage—step two—it was up to him to save his daughter's life. I had interrupted his habitual pattern of attacking his ex-wife—step three. I had defined the problem in solvable terms—step four—stopping the war was something that he could do. I had created an empowering alternative—step five—loving Joan because she was Beth's mother. I had given him a plan that he could put into action—step six—what he would actually express and do. And I had related all this to a higher purpose—step seven—being a protector and the one who would save his daughter's life.)

He said, incredulously, "Then Beth will eat?"

"Yes," I said.

He did it, and Beth began to eat. Very soon she was at a normal weight, and I helped in getting her readmitted to the private school from which she had been expelled due to the anorexia.

It's All about Love

Jason, an 80-year-old man, consulted me about his forty-something son, Fred, who was a cocaine addict. Jason had just paid for Fred's 1-month stay at a residential treatment center, and he was due to get out in a few days. Jason and the rest of the family were afraid Fred would go back to his old ways once he was released, and they were desperate to prevent that. I decided it would be best to meet with the entire family.

After Jason finished his treatment, the family arrived en masse. The tension between them was something to behold. During his cocaine binges, Fred had done some pretty awful things. In addition to the typical sexual adventures, infidelities, and financial disasters, he had also been arrested for public nudity as well as an assortment of other drug-induced behaviors that he could neither remember nor explain.

Accompanying Fred to the meeting were Jason and his former wife, Margaret; Fred's brothers and sisters; his wife, Constance; and his two teenage sons. It was a big, conflicted group. Before they even began, I could see evidence of tremendous contempt on Fred's sons' faces. They resented their father and immediately made their feelings known.

I realized I had to take a completely different approach with this family, given the tension in the room. So I began by telling them that what is important in a family is love. I wanted to divert their focus from Fred and his addiction, so I asked them to talk to one another about pleasant memories from the past. I wanted them to talk about their love for one another. I wanted them to share how they had loved previously and how they would love one another in the future. I asked them how they could continue to support one another during these difficult times.

Everything was going pretty well until Fred said something that annoyed one of his sons. Both boys acted indignant in chorus, started screaming at Fred, called him a lowlife who had ruined their lives, and stomped out of the room. I calmly asked Jason to go retrieve his grandsons and bring them back.

I had arranged the session around a conference table, as if they were all attending a business meeting, hoping this would reduce the emotional fireworks. Once the teenage boys were resettled at the table, admittedly fuming, I asked Jason and Margaret to talk to one another about the ways they still loved one another. It was clear to everyone in the room that they still held one another in high regard and affection even with their estrangement (and remarriages) over the years. I emphasized how much they loved one another even though they couldn't live together.

The others present watched the interaction with rapt attention. The boys, in particular, were amazed to hear their grandparents speaking to one another with such tenderness. Fred and Constance were obviously moved by the conversation, even inspired to join in with talk about their own mutual love. Throughout the meeting, whenever any of the participants lapsed into old habits of complaint or accusation, I gently led them back to talk about love.

Constance had come into the session prepared to announce that she was filing for divorce, that she'd had enough of her husband's antics and self-destructive behavior. After hearing her in-laws speak about their lingering love for one another, she felt more willing to rethink her decision. She agreed that Fred could move back into the house and would sleep in the guest room. The two sons rolled their eyes at this, but they were clearly pleased. The session ended with an agreement that they would return in a few months.

I didn't hear from then again until 19 months later. Fred had been completely clean all those months. Constance was suspicious that Fred might be using again. I recommended that they continue regular drug testing.

What had sustained Fred during this time, making it possible for him to remain free of drugs? It was the talk about love that changed their relationship in a way that could contain him in the family and keep him in the home. I have no doubt that if Constance had expelled him, he would have gone back to drugs.

A Novel Solution

I received an e-mail from a friend of a friend who desperately wanted a consultation, but she wouldn't really say what it was about. All she would say was that it involved a problem with her marriage.

Josh and Natalie arrived at my office exactly on time for their appointment. Natalie was a very stylish woman in her forties, impeccably dressed and made up. Josh was big and round, like a football player gone to seed. Their manners were just as different as their appearances. Natalie was serious, almost severe, while Josh was jovial.

They had no children, were solid financially, and told me they had a good marriage—they were best friends. They enjoyed many activities together and had a really great relationship.

"So, what's the problem then?" I asked.

"Well," Natalie started, then looked at Josh to see if he was going to interject anything.

"Yes?" I encouraged her to keep going.

"Well, it's . . . it's hard to talk about."

"Is it something to do with sex?" I've worked with many married couples; this was hardly a shot in the dark.

"Well, kind of," Natalie answered, looking even more uncomfortable. Josh had looked up from his shirt and was grinning.

"Kind of?"

Natalie nodded but didn't speak. I looked at Josh, hoping he might help out, but it was clear he was sitting this one out.

"Okay," I tried again, "is it some kind of performance problem between you?"

"Uh, no, not exactly," Natalie answered.

"I see. How about problems having orgasms, something like that?"

Natalie looked on the verge of bolting out of the room, she was so uncomfortable. But she shook her head and said under her breath, "No, not that either."

"How about infidelity?" I was running out of guesses. "Are one or both of you having affairs?"

Jackpot! Natalie began nodding her head vigorously. "Yes," she said, but at the exact same moment that Josh said, "No!"

I was confused. "One of you is saying that there is infidelity, and the other is saying no. What's going on?"

Josh turned to his wife. "Come on now," he said to her, "you can't say I had an affair. I never had an affair."

"No," Natalie said, her anger rising, "but you had sex."

"How can you say that? We never had intercourse."

"Well, it was sexual, wasn't it?"

"Not really. I never even spoke to the woman."

I was more confused than ever. Natalie was accusing her husband of having an affair, which he was denying. Apparently, he was with a woman, and they had sex—but they didn't have sex. Sounded like a president I'd heard of.

"Hold on, hold on," I interrupted them. "Josh, you were with a woman? Is that what Natalie was saying?"

Josh hesitated, then nodded.

"How many times would that be?"

"How many times was I with her?"

"Exactly."

"Oh, many times, I'd say."

"Okay. So you were with this woman many times. You never spoke to her. You never had intercourse. But you did have sex. Or you didn't have sex."

Natalie began crying, seeming to break the evasive spell. Finally, Josh explained that he had a sexual preference for sadomasochistic sex and he had been seeing a dominatrix. From time to time he would seek the services of a specialist in chains and whips, dressed in black leather and high-heeled boots. He would pay her to beat him, ending in masturbation. So, technically, he had been correct in saying that they never spoke to one another except in the form of commands that his dominatrix would issue, nor did they ever touch one another.

When Natalie had first discovered her husband's proclivities, she tried to play the domineering role herself. But her heart wasn't in it, and Josh said she didn't satisfy him the same way as his hired specialist. To add to their problems, Natalie had an important position in the community, and she had just learned that Josh had done something incredibly, spectacularly stupid that might jeopardize her career. Natalie had launched an investigation to gather evidence against an employee who had been engaging in unethical if not illegal behavior in the company. As fate would have it, at the same time Josh had put an advertisement on a Web site, including a nude photo of himself (big belly and all) looking for someone who might dominate him for the pure pleasure. And guess who applied for the job? The same woman who Natalie was trying to fire!

Josh and the woman met several times to play their sadomasochistic games, during which the woman was gathering evidence to blackmail her way into keeping her job. She showed up at Natalie's office armed with nude photos of Josh. It was this latest crisis that had led them to seek my help.

It was one of my wilder challenges. I knew I was going to have to be very creative to help this couple, but inspiration was with me, and I came up with a plan.

"I know what you need to do," I told them, "and it's really up to you whether you want to do it or not, but it is really the only solution you have to get yourselves out of this mess. The solution is *not* for your husband to give up his sexual preference." I was careful to use neutral language and stay away from words like "perversion."

"It isn't?" Natalie blurted.

"No, that's not the answer."

When he heard that, Josh grinned.

"Well then," Natalie said, "what then? I don't want to lose my husband. I love him. . . ." She looked at him. " . . . In spite of everything. We have so many good things together."

"The only solution, then, is for you to join him in his sexual preference."

"But we already tried that," she said. "I tried to . . ."

"Yes, yes, I know. But I have something quite different in mind."

"You do?"

"Yes. From now on, you are going to be the one in charge."

"In charge?"

"Yes. What Josh is doing is potentially very dangerous with all the whips and things. He could be injured. So you need to make sure that he is safe."

I had Natalie's attention. Josh's smile was gone.

"I want you to find Josh a dominatrix who is both safe and legal. You're going to research this and find the right person for him, someone he would enjoy, yet someone you trust. Make sense?"

It *did* make sense to Natalie.

"Then," I continued, "I want you to be present at all times. You are going to be the one to pay this person, and you are going to stay in the room to make sure that your husband is safe. You have to make sure that he doesn't get in trouble or do anything that you'd consider inappropriate."

Josh clearly needed variety; Natalie clearly needed certainty. Clearly, they loved one another. I knew they would react either straightforwardly or paradoxically. If they complied with my instructions, then they would share a sexual life together that, although a rather unusual one, would keep them intimately engaged, and Natalie could have some control. If, on the other hand, one or both of them (most likely Josh) began to dislike this activity, it would work to end future indulgence. Either way, there was potentially a satisfactory solution. I wasn't 100 percent sure that this solution would work, but I could see that Natalie truly loved Josh and wanted to stay in the marriage. Since she had already tried to play the dominatrix to Josh in the past, and she had even shown anger about it, I thought it might well work.

A few months later, I met with Josh and Natalie again. Their new arrangement was working. Natalie had found a new dominatrix who was also a personal trainer. It seems she had a plan to get her chubby husband to lose weight at the same time he indulged in his sexual fantasies. Under Natalie's instructions, the dominatrix was using her resources to motivate Josh's exercise program, literally pursuing him on a treadmill with the whip at his butt. It was working, too. Josh was losing weight, even though he complained he didn't like mixing work with pleasure.

At one point, Josh injured himself during a session. There were actually very strict rules and "safe signals" during domination activities to ensure that nobody was injured. But now Josh found himself being ordered around not only by the dominatrix but also by his wife, and told to run faster, lift harder, do this or that.

"Why didn't you just tell them to stop, use your safe word?" I asked him.

"I tried to," he said. "I told them it was too hard, but they didn't listen. The two of them—they're friends now—and they kind of ganged up on me. I just couldn't tell them to stop. I had two women ordering me around, and I couldn't say no."

This was fantastic. The beauty of the paradoxical reaction. "I see," I said, seeing all too clearly.

"So, how are you feeling now?"

"Are you kidding? I've got bruises for God's sake! And I'm so sore I can barely walk."

Josh went on to declare that he had lost interest in the dominatrix.

I asked Natalie to apologize to Josh for not realizing that the boot camp experience was too much for him. Then I asked Josh to admit that he had to accept some responsibility for not telling the women he'd had enough. Then I sent them off to discover other fun things that they could do together. I'm waiting to hear from them. I can't wait to hear what they try next!

Chapter 8

HELPLESSNESS
IS POWERFUL

Psychologist Martin Seligman, author of *Learned Optimism*, has described the patterns of beliefs that cause us to feel helpless.[1] They are:

1. Believing in the permanence of a problem. A typical example is the thought "I am depressed. I will always suffer from this condition."

2. Believing in the pervasiveness of a problem: "This child is not very intelligent. He will always fail."

3. Believing in the personal nature of a problem: "As a mother, I'm not strong enough or knowledgeable enough to help my child to change."

Holding these limiting beliefs is equivalent to gradually poisoning yourself. With too many challenges, however, many people begin to experience their efforts as futile and ultimately develop learned helplessness.

Not only are we set up for failure by learned helplessness, so are those we care about.

Who's in Charge?

At first glance, it seems that there is no question as to who are the powerful and who are the helpless. As we've seen before, in human relationships weakness can be a source of power. The great religious and political leaders have always understood this.

The reality is that the powerful are powerful *and* helpless at the same time; the helpless are helpless *and* powerful simultaneously. Carl Jung called this "the cruciform nature of reality." Everything in our experience is composed of opposites, and these opposites are not simply pairs of polarities, such as light and dark, male and female. Rather, existence is comprised of antinomies that are internally consistent, mutually exclusive truths.[2]

Nowhere is the irrational, paradoxical nature of human relationships more apparent than in marriage—a relationship that is entered into voluntarily and that severely limits our freedom. As the spouses try to maintain some independence from each other, they struggle with the issue of sharing power. Power refers to the possibility not only of dominating the other but also of comforting, reforming, taking care of, and taking responsibility for the other person.

Different couples divide areas of control, power, and responsibility in different ways. One spouse may make all the decisions having to do with home and children, while the other spouse makes all the decisions involving the social context outside the family. In another marriage, one spouse may have power over all the decisions involving money, while the other spouse may make all the decisions involving family and friends.

When couples struggle because each wants to have control over the same area, the struggle may be resolved by deriving power from helplessness. Both spouses may capitulate to an adolescent child, who makes them equal by dominating both of them. One spouse may make most of the decisions in the family, but the other spouse may side with the children in a way that undermines the decision-making spouse. Sometimes, a "personal problem," instead of a child, becomes a source of power. Problems such as depression, alcoholism, drug addiction, anxiety, and physical illness may serve this purpose.

In ongoing relationships, interactions repeat over time and become part of a system so that each participant knows what to expect. For example, a wife might expect her husband to call, "Honey, I'm home," every day as he walks through the door and to greet her with a kiss. The husband might expect the wife to ask, "How was your day?" and to have dinner ready. A system of interaction consists of such interchanges as well as the expectations that each spouse has of the other.

When one of the spouses develops a "personal problem," a system of interaction develops around the problem. This system of interaction becomes an analogy or a metaphor for the original struggle that the couple could not resolve. The personal problem itself may be a metaphor (for example, a husband with a pain in the neck may be indicating that the wife is a pain in the neck), and the way the couple deals with the problem (the pain) is a metaphor for the way they deal with other issues.[3]

A Literal and Metaphoric Headache

Peter and Mary have been married for 10 years. Both worked when they were married, but Mary left her job 6 years ago when Mitchell was born. Now Mitchell is in school. Since Peter now makes all the income in the family, he has long felt that Mary should be thriftier—and especially not spend so much money on clothes for herself and Mitchell. So Peter for 6 years has been trying to cajole Mary to spend less money. For the past year, since Mitchell has begun school, Peter has been trying to motivate Mary to find a job. The struggle has become so severe that the marriage is threatened: Peter feels he's carrying too much weight, and Mary feels all her work in the home and with Mitchell is unappreciated. And Peter has become more and more controlling about money. The inequality between them has become intolerable.

Mary has become depressed and developed incapacitating headaches. The headaches are Mary's "personal problem." Now Peter tries to motivate Mary to come out of her depression—to seek medical treatment for the headaches, see a therapist, consider taking an antidepressant—instead of trying to influence her to save money and find work, which are the issues that they could not resolve. The system of interaction that develops around Mary's depression and headaches is an analogy for other systems of interaction in the marriage. The interaction around Mary's personal problem makes it possible for Peter and Mary to know where each stands in relation to the other without having to explicitly discuss the issues of money and work that were endangering the marriage.

Let's look at the sequence of events. In their marriage, Peter is dominant; his career is considered more important than Mary's role as homemaker and mother. Peter makes most of the decisions about how money should be spent, where they live, what car to buy, where to vacation, and so forth. Then he starts nagging Mary to be thriftier or to get a part-time job. A few months later, Mary becomes depressed and develops headaches. By becoming a "personal-problem spouse," Mary gives even more power to Peter, who tries to motivate Mary to get rid of the problem and who, in contrast to Mary, appears even more adequate and competent.

However, Peter fails repeatedly to motivate Mary or to solve her problem. It is tacitly implied that Peter should solve the problem somehow, that the very existence of the problem is Peter's responsibility. Also, Peter now has a number of things to do for Mary, or instead of Mary. When her headaches are really bad, he has to cook and care for Mitchell. Peter is deprived of doing a number of other things because of Mary's problem—she doesn't like to entertain or to go out dancing, and isn't much interested in sex. In this way, becoming a personal-problem spouse gives power to Mary over Peter.

The system of interaction around Mary's personal problem is analogous to the system of interaction around other issues in Peter's and Mary's lives. That is, Peter and Mary interact around Mary's personal problem in ways that are analogical to the way they interact around issues of Mary's spending and failure to find a part-time job. Peter tells Mary what to do about her depression and headaches and complains because Mary is not motivated to seek help, or not the kind of help Peter thinks she needs. Mary complains that what Peter wants her to do is not right. If Peter were more interested, or sensitive, or understanding, or involved, Mary would feel better or would be more motivated to change.

In this way, Peter and Mary discuss Peter's dominant position and Mary's unhappiness with their situation while talking about her personal problem. Mary expresses, through her depression and headaches, both the intention of not being dominated as well as the helplessness of her situation. Peter's position as the spouse of a personal-problem spouse constitutes both his power and his helplessness. If Mary overcomes her depression, Peter and Mary will go back to struggling about whether Mary should find a part-time job or over whether Peter should determine how money should be spent. As these issues do not get resolved, Mary will develop another personal problem, and the cycle will be repeated.

Sometimes a child will develop a problem and save the spouse from becoming a personal-problem spouse. If this happens to Peter and Mary, they will focus on Mitchell's problem in the same way they previously focused on Mary's. For example, Mitchell may develop problems at school, refusing to go along with the group, teasing other children, and being generally disruptive in class. Peter and Mary will both come together in trying to motivate Mitchell to be cooperative at school, but they will disagree on how to do this. Peter might insist on punishments, while Mary may want to try positive reinforcement and reward Mitchell for staying out of trouble. Peter and Mary's interaction around the child's problem will become a metaphor for their interaction around their other difficulties. That is, there may be a cyclical variation in the focus of interaction (sometimes they will focus on Peter's career, sometimes on the issue of money, sometimes on Mary's depression, sometimes on Mitchell's problems at school), but the cycle of interaction will remain the same. Peter will continue to try to motivate Mary to get help for her personal problems, while Mary will continue to want a more egalitarian relationship.

The following example illustrates the cycle and shows how Danielle developed a personal problem, how her behavior can best be understood in the context of her relationship with Ralph, and how Ralph can change so Danielle is motivated to change.

The Wicked Stepmother

Danielle was a naturally attractive woman with long, brown curly hair and enormous brown eyes. Her manner was sweet, and she seemed to be sensitive and kind. Her husband, Ralph, began to talk about their marriage and the difficulties they had been through in emigrating from Chile. As they moved on to talk about the problem that had brought them to me, it was hard to believe that Danielle was rejecting a little child.

As she referred to the joint custody arrangement that Ralph had with his first wife, Danielle said, "I feel like I live in a jail." Having Ralph's little daughter with them half of the time made Danielle feel like a prisoner.

I was puzzled. The child, Sabrina, was only 5 years old, and both spouses agreed that she was extremely well behaved.

I asked, "Danielle, do you understand how your husband suffers because he has married a woman who won't accept his child?" Danielle nodded, and I asked her to turn to her husband and tell him that she understood his suffering.

Instead Danielle said, "I can't accept it. I have trouble accepting that he has a daughter and we can't be free." Incongruently, she kissed him on the cheek and added, "I love you and I want us to be happy."

I asked, "But do you understand that this is painful to him?"

"I understand," said Danielle. "I know."

"You won't have a real marriage until you accept that his daughter is part of him," I told her.

Ralph explained that he didn't want to have children with Danielle until she accepted Sabrina. Danielle said she didn't want to have children until she could feel comfortable in her own home. She added, "We can't continue together, we can't live together while I feel the way I do, and this is not the way I want to feel. I don't want it. That's why we came to therapy."

I was stumped. Why did Danielle reject the child if she didn't want to do so? What was the original struggle that had led to Danielle rejecting a child as her "personal problem"? A clue to determining when a particular behavior or emotion constitutes a "personal problem" is that it is presented as involuntary behavior, out of the control of the person. Danielle's rejection of Sabrina was clearly her personal problem. But why?

Danielle went on to explain that in the last year Sabrina had developed a nervous cough. She coughed constantly. One day recently, Danielle had been in a good mood and had a good day with Sabrina, and she didn't cough at all. "When she doesn't feel that rejection from me, she's happy and she doesn't cough, and then my husband is happy also," said Danielle.

I thought, "This woman is insufferable," but I said something quite different: "Sabrina loves you."

"She does," they both said.

"You punish each other," I said. "Danielle, you punish Ralph by rejecting Sabrina, and he punishes you by refusing to have children with you. Tell him again that you understand his pain."

"I can say it," said Danielle, "but I don't feel it."

"I'm confused. How can you not feel that he suffers? You're a kind, loving woman. How can you say you don't feel it?"

"I don't know how to explain it."

"You've told me that Sabrina is a good, sweet child."

"Yes."

"How can you not be fond of her?"

"I'm fond of her, but she interferes in my life."

"How?"

Danielle told of a recent incident when she had wanted them to spend a day at the beach with her brother and his children, without Sabrina. She said, "I know that I married Ralph and he has a daughter, but why can't we spend a day with my family without his daughter?"

"If she were the daughter of the two of you, you wouldn't even consider not including her."

"That's right," said Ralph.

"If she were my daughter, I wouldn't exclude her," said Danielle.

"That's right," I said. "You wouldn't exclude her from any family events."

"Why do I feel like this?" Danielle asked me. "Because it's real, I feel it."

"You haven't accepted that Sabrina is part of your family."

"No, I don't feel that she's part of my family."

"Then he isn't part of your family either," I said, pointing to Ralph.

"Yes, he's my family," said Danielle.

"Impossible," I said. "This man is part of a package; he is not childless." I turned to Ralph, "I'm going to ask you now, Ralph, to say to Danielle that you demand that she treat Sabrina as if she were her child, that Sabrina is part of the family and cannot be excluded from family activities."

"That's why she's giving you this example," said Ralph, "because we had a fight about it. I said, 'Sabrina is coming on the weekend. Why would we separate her from the family group?' It wasn't like we were going to a nightclub—it was an outing with children."

"Can you tell her now?"

Danielle and Ralph laughed nervously. "I can tell her," he said, shrugging his shoulders helplessly.

"You have to accept Sabrina," he said. "She is part of our family."

"What do I have to do now?" Danielle asked me.

"I ask you, please," begged Ralph.

"I don't know what I have to do," Danielle shrugged.

"If you don't say something, you're rejecting him," I said. "You have to accept his request."

Danielle turned to Ralph, "Okay, yes, I accept it. But I don't feel it!"

The conversation was not going well. I decided to take the issue to the very basis of a marital relationship—the marital vows. "The two of you take your marriage seriously, don't you?" I began.

Ralph interrupted, "Yes, I take it so seriously that that's why I'm asking for help. I'm here because I'm lost."

I tried to say something, but Danielle talked right over me, "Ralph sometimes treats me as if I were a little girl. There's no difference with Sabrina—even the names. He calls Sabrina 'Bugsy,' and I'm 'Bugsy,' too. I'm not Bugsy. I don't like him to call me Bugsy."

"Precisely," I said, "because you are a mature woman, you have to see the reality of the situation, which is that Sabrina is Ralph's and your daughter."

"She's not my daughter," interrupted Danielle with indignation.

"She's your stepdaughter. Ralph loves her, and when he calls you by the same nickname, he's showing you the same love he feels for her."

"I don't like it. I want my love, not someone else's."

I realized I needed to go deeper. I had to remind the couple that marriage is about love. "We need to talk about love because marriage is about love, and it is the deep love that you have for each other that has brought you here today, so marital therapy also has to be about love. Without love there is nothing. And love is confirmed with actions. Sometimes actions come first, and they lead to love." Addressing Danielle, I continued, "You didn't bond with Sabrina from birth because you were not the biological mother. So now, what I would like you to do is every time you are with Sabrina, I would like you to plan some loving action, small things to do with her that will mean love. The goal is to develop the love."

The talk of love worked its magic. Suddenly, Danielle's manner changed. Her tone was strict and pained as she said, "I want to tell you something. I enjoyed Sabrina very much when I first came into Ralph's life. I taught her to talk. We spent a lot of time together. But something affected me very much. Sabrina started school, and I helped her with her schoolwork. I enjoyed it. When the school party came around, the mother said that if I went, she wouldn't go. So everything I had given Sabrina, all my love, that day they told me: 'That's it.' Do you understand?"

Finally, I understood. As soon as I had begun to talk about love, Danielle remembered her love for Sabrina and her suffering when she was excluded and slighted. It's a great pain to love a child who belongs to somebody else. By rejecting Sabrina, Danielle was protecting herself from further suffering, even at the cost of her marital happiness, and even though she was making Sabrina suffer.

"That was a big mistake," I said to Ralph, "not to insist that your ex-wife accept Danielle's part in Sabrina's life."

"I did insist," said Ralph. "I had an argument with her, and she said, 'If Danielle comes, I won't go.'"

"So he said, 'Fine,'" said Danielle.

"That has changed now," said Ralph.

"It changed because she now has a boyfriend, and she wants him to participate. It didn't change because Ralph did anything to make it change," added Danielle.

"I think, Ralph, that you have to apologize to Danielle for not having done anything to change this situation," I said.

"I've apologized 20 times, and I'll apologize a thousand times more," he turned to Danielle. "I didn't have bad intentions. I just thought it would be ugly for the mother not to go." Turning to me, "I asked Danielle as my wife, 'Please do it for Sabrina, make the sacrifice.' Maybe I was wrong."

"Tell her," I said.

Ralph turned to Danielle, "Maybe I was wrong; forgive me."

"It can never happen again that anyone questions the role of your wife, and you have only one wife, and that's Danielle," I said.

"It won't happen again," said Ralph.

"Do you believe him?" I asked Danielle.

She opened her eyes wide and shrugged, "I hope so. I always feel that I'm in and I'm out. Nobody gives me my place."

"What would Ralph have to do for you to believe him?"

"Simply that the next time we're in a similar situation, I want to feel that I'm his wife."

"Tell him precisely what he has to do."

"If it happens again that she calls and says, 'Danielle isn't going,' you say, 'Danielle is going,' and that's it. That's what I want." It was clear that she was deeply hurt and feared giving love to Sabrina and being rejected again. "With respect to the activities with Sabrina," she continued, turning to me, "it's hard for me to be giving now. But we used to do lots of things. The other day I was in a good mood, and I had her working with me at my desk, and she was very happy."

"So you sincerely love her," I said.

"I do, but I found that maybe distancing myself would be better for me. I felt I gave a lot, and then I felt used."

I turned to Ralph, "I will give you a suggestion as to what you can do to announce to the world that this woman is your wife. You will call your parents and affirm to them that this is the woman you want to be with all your life. It was an error not to marry her first." Turning to Danielle I added, "Would this make you feel good?"

"I know part of Ralph's family loves me," said Danielle, gesturing quotation marks in the air, "but they don't accept me."

I asked Ralph, "They don't accept that you married a second time?"

"They're strange, difficult," he answered. "But Danielle, they did accept you from the start."

"It's not how I feel," Danielle said. "I could say Ralph's mother loves me, but I feel there is something there, something hidden—that's why I'm here. You know, I talk to his mother, we communicate, but maybe what I need is for Ralph to say to her, 'Danielle is my wife. She's the one I love.' That's what I need."

Danielle was beginning to address the original problem, asserting herself and coming out of her personal-problem spouse position. She turned to Ralph, "And say it to your sister, too, that I am your wife."

"And also to your ex-wife," I said.

"Yes," said Ralph.

"So, you loved Sabrina, and you suffered when you distanced yourself." The story was now quite different from the one the couple was telling when they first came into my office.

"Yes," said Danielle, "I had to deliberately make the effort to distance myself."

"Ralph, you have to make three phone calls," I said. Danielle laughed. "One to your mother, one to your father, and one to your ex-wife. To each you have to say that Danielle is your wife and you love her, and what a good mother she is to Sabrina. How she taught her to speak, all the good things they did together." Ralph nodded in agreement. "And there's a fourth phone call to your sister." I turned to Danielle, "You know, Danielle, you've done so much for Sabrina. You taught her to speak; did you teach her to read also?"

"No, because by then I already was into this stuff." A good sign that Danielle was leaving her "personal problem" behind was that now she referred to it as "stuff."

"What else did you do with her?"

"Cooking," said Danielle. "To knit and to sew," added Ralph almost simultaneously.

"I used to spend entire days with her," said Danielle, "and I loved it. I enjoyed her very much."

"Ralph, you caused Danielle to lose that love for Sabrina, and you caused all the suffering that went with that loss."

"Whenever we are with family or friends," said Danielle, "they all talk to Ralph about Sabrina. They praise her to him only, as if I had nothing to do with her, as if I didn't exist."

"You have to change that, Ralph. Here is a phone. I want you to call your ex-wife right now and tell her how much you appreciate Danielle, how good she is with Sabrina."

"Yes," said Ralph and reached for the phone. Danielle smiled broadly and sighed. Ralph talked into the phone: "Hello, hi, I'm calling to tell you that I love Danielle very much, that she's a very good mother for Sabrina, she loves her very much. *(Pause)* I just wanted to tell you. She does the best she can for Sabrina. *(Pause)* I just wanted to reaffirm this. *(Pause)* There is a special reason. I'm in a therapy session, and they proposed this idea of talking to you, and I'm doing it because I think it's the right thing. *(Pause)* There have been certain differences with respect to the party at Sabrina's school that Danielle couldn't go. That won't happen again. *(Pause)* Okay, I'll talk to you later, bye."

As he put down the phone, Danielle put her arms around his neck and kissed him on the lips. She remained hugging him, her head on his shoulder and her arms around him. Then she rubbed his arm gently and kissed him on the shoulder. Looking deeply into his eyes, she whispered, "Thank you." They kissed again, and Danielle continued to hold him, caressing his arm and gazing into his eyes. He whispered something to her.

I asked Ralph to make a similar phone call to his mother in South America. He did, and Danielle once again hugged and kissed him.

From then on, Danielle became a loving second mother to Sabrina, behaving as if she had never been estranged from her.

Strategy for Change

How could it be that Ralph believed he had been doing everything he could think of during the course of more than a year to motivate Danielle to be kind to Sabrina but he had failed—and in one session, because of two phone calls, everything changed? The answer is that Danielle was part of a system of interaction. She and Sabrina did not have a relationship that was separate from other family members, any more than Danielle and Ralph could have a relationship separate from Sabrina. For Danielle to change, Ralph had to change his relationship with his ex-wife and with his mother, and he had to do so in Danielle's presence, asserting that Danielle had the right to a relationship with Sabrina. No attempts to motivate Danielle to behave differently had succeeded, and yet two brief phone calls brought about the change.

The motivational strategy could be expressed in this way: If A wants to motivate B to change in relation to C, then A has to change in relation to D and E. When the relationship between A, D, and E changes, then the relationship between B and C has to change. Another way of saying this is: If Ralph is close to Danielle, to Sabrina, to his ex-wife, and to his mother, and he wants Danielle and Sabrina to be closer to each other, he has to pull away from his ex-wife and his mother, and become closer to Danielle and Sabrina. Then, in turn, Danielle and Sabrina can be closer to each other.[4]

Drop Dead, Witch

Here's another story that illustrates how breaking a pattern of interaction can reverse years of conflict and suffering. Here, too, you'll see the power of changing the focus by doing something really different, something that may even sound absurd, even cruel, to shake a couple out of their pattern.

Marianne had undergone 10 years of therapy without success. She had panic attacks that started early in the morning and were often accompanied by intestinal cramps and diarrhea. At those times she thought about her own death and was overwhelmed by the fear of dying. Her long-suffering, sympathetic, handsome husband, Marc, had done everything in his power to help her, but to no avail. Because of her "personal problem," Marianne couldn't take care of the house or the children, so her mother and her mother-in-law took turns and did everything for her. Once in a while, Marianne made an attempt to do something, for example, to go to the grocery store, but she was always overwhelmed by panic.

Dr. Chouhy, an expert in family problems, was asked by Marianne's current therapist to consult with the couple. He asked Marc how he had attempted to help Marianne, and Marc described how he listened to her, talked to her, gave her love, and took care of her in every way. Chouhy listened carefully and then said, "Perhaps it's time to do something differently."

"Like what?" asked Marc. "I'm willing to do anything to solve this problem."

"Since what you have been doing hasn't been working, perhaps we should consider doing something that is quite the opposite, don't you think?"

"Yes," said Marc, puzzled.

"What do you typically say to Marianne before you leave for work in the morning?" asked Chouhy.

"I tell her that I love her, and I say I hope she feels better and has a better day."

"Mm-hmm. What could you say that would be the opposite of that?"

"That I don't love her."

"That's good, but I want something really strong, really awful. What could it be?"

"I could say, 'Drop dead!'" said Marc.

Marianne gasped in shocked but amused surprise.

"That's good, very good. Now something even stronger."

"Drop dead, Witch! Once and for all, drop dead!"

"Very good. Anything else you could add?"

"Yes," said Marc, turning to Marianne, "and if you die, I'm marrying again!"

"I don't think this is very nice," said Marianne, "and I don't see how anything like this could work."

"Every morning, before you go to work," said Chouhy, "I want you to say to Marianne, 'Drop dead, Witch, and if you die, I'm marrying again!' And you must say it with feeling. Can you do that?"

"Yes, I can," said Marc, smiling mischievously at Marianne.

"This is a rude way of talking, and it won't help me," said Marianne to Chouhy.

"I want you to do it every morning for a couple of weeks, and we'll see." Chouhy looked at Marianne, "You know it's time for something different."

They left and a few days later Chouhy got an emergency phone call late at night from Marc. Marianne had become very upset, screamed at her mother and mother-in-law, and carried on about dying in such a way that the whole family was scared. Chouhy invited everyone, including the two grandmothers, to come in to see him the next morning.

By the time they arrived, Marianne was completely composed. She explained to Chouhy that Marc had told her to drop dead, called her witch and so forth every morning, and it has made her think about her situation. So it was time to tell the truth.

She proceeded to explain that both she and Marc came from very traditional Italian families. Marianne had always wanted to study and to work, but when she was married, she was told by both her mother and her mother-in-law that she was expected to take care of her husband, the home, and the children, and nothing else. She resented this deeply but said nothing. Turning to the two grandmothers she said firmly, "It's over now. I'm going back to school, and that's it." The two women, Marc, and the children reassured her that that would be perfectly fine with them. Two years later, Marianne was doing well in school, was happy in her marriage, and the panic had never recurred.

Marianne had been punishing the two grandmothers, her husband, herself, and her children because of her resentment at the limitations imposed by the previous generation. Instead of rebelling and asserting herself, she had become a personal-problem spouse, involved almost exclusively in her suffering. The husband had turned to comforting her and accepting the way she was without any demands or criticism, and so had the two grandmothers. When Marc was able to criticize her for the first time, and to do so in an exaggerated, intense way, he broke his own habitual pattern for dealing with Marianne and so enabled her to break her habitual pattern of illness and misery. After a short initial phase of being even more upset and miserable, Marianne herself realized what she had to do, and she changed her life.

Chapter 9

RECOVERING FROM LOSS

There is no way to avoid loss. But it is important not to let mourning take over our lives, not to let a great loss lead us into prolonged despair and helplessness.

Every one of us has someone or something about which we care so deeply that our identity, our self-esteem, and even our sense of self is tied to it. For most people, it is a relationship with a spouse, a partner, a child, a family member, or even a special friend. But for others, their position in the world can define who they are: their position in the community, at work, even their financial success. The loss of any of these can threaten the bedrock of our identity, jeopardize our relationships, and throw us into despair.

All of us, in the course of our lives, will face circumstances that seem difficult, even impossible to withstand. But withstand them we must. I hope to show you that while catastrophic events are a source of great pain, they can also bring out the best in you, and help you to create an even more compelling future for yourself and others.

What would happen if you lost your husband, your partner, your mother, your child, your job, your house, your investments, your friends, or your health, which allows you to maintain your lifestyle and community activities? Some people refuse to even think about what they would do if faced with such losses. Others immediately start to think about solutions: They see an opportunity to rise to a challenge and spring to alertness and action.

Still others look at the prospect of loss as an opportunity to make major shifts in their lives. Loss can be a true test of who you really are, what you value, and what you're capable of.

When we lose someone or something that feels essential to our well-being, we experience great pain and stress. Our model of the world is threatened, and we no longer know how we'll meet our fundamental needs. And when we cannot meet our needs, we experience a crisis. The loss leading to a crisis could be the loss of a loved one, the closing of a business, the loss of a job, relocation to another city or country, or the loss of a business partner.

Recovering a Lost Memory

A grieving woman named Maggie once stood up at a Tony Robbins event. She said, "I didn't realize that for the last 8 years, I've been struggling to try to give my son's death some meaning. What I was really having a difficult time facing is my biggest fear—the fear of failure. And the ultimate failure for a mother is not being able to protect her child."[1]

A parent who loses a child feels that they could have better protected the child and that, since the child has died, they have failed. Parents feel this even when there is no possible way that they could have prevented the death. It's not a logical reaction, but it is an emotional one that can ruin a life.

Maggie's son, Leonard, had died at age 17 in a freak accident.

"What would Leonard want for you?" Tony asked.

"He would want me to be happy right now."

"How unhappy would his spirit be, would his soul be, seeing you the way you've been for the last 8 years?"

"He would be tormented."

"What was one of the funniest things he ever said to you?"

Maggie replied, imitating a teenage boy, "Are you really going to go out like that?" She laughed, and the audience laughed.

Tony said, "He's talking about your life for the last 8 years." Tony's comment located the woman's son in the present, in a position of observing and advising his mother.

When we lose an important source of love, one way we hold onto it is to connect with it out of a feeling of pain, guilt, or regret. Although Maggie could not have prevented her son's death, she was still beating herself up about it as though this would prolong her identity as a mother. She needed to find new ways of connecting with her son.

"Do you have a spiritual or a religious belief?" Tony asked.

"I believe in God."

"Do you believe in the hereafter?"

"Yes, I do."

"Do you believe your boy is still vibrant?"

"Yes, I do."

"With your eyes closed, Maggie, I want you to feel him holding you, kissing you on the top of the head, and then looking into your eyes. Feel his presence completely. You let me know when his presence is completely with you."

After a short pause Maggie said, "He's right here in front of me."

"I want you to listen carefully to what he's going to say," said Tony. "Because what he's going to say will not only free you, but it will also remind you forever of what is the truth. Listen carefully now as he tells you the truth that will set you free."

Whenever people get stuck in a position of helplessness and grief, there is always an answer that they have not been listening to. Tony knew that Maggie already had the answer that would set her free and that it would be most healing for her to receive the answer through the voice of her son.

"Feel the depth of what he's telling you," Tony went on, "that sets you free in every cell in your body. Not just in your head, like you were a moment ago, but in your heart, in your soul, in your spirit, your hands, your feet, your smile, your eyes. Ears hearing, eyes that now have insight, not just sight. Feel the strength he sends into you, the strength you knew he always had and now he feels. Can you feel his strength? Hear what he's saying to you, and let it pierce you. Hear the truth. And as you start to take in the truth, watch him begin to smile when you begin to truly take in the truth. What did your son tell you?"

"That I'm a beautiful free spirit that needs to be out there."

"How big did he smile?"

"I saw him smiling, which I don't see very often any more."

"How could he smile when you've been beating yourself up for 8 years? Would you be smiling if he was miserable for 8 straight years?"

"No."

"Beating himself up as if he did something to you. Is he also more whole now?"

"Very much so."

"I would like you now to put both hands on your heart and breathe deeply," said Tony. "And as you breathe into your heart, I want you to imagine all of your son's love and his wicked sense of humor."

Maggie laughed, and Tony said, "He has a wicked sense of humor, doesn't he? I want you to experience all that wicked sense of humor and his love inside of you. And as you breathe into your heart, I want you to feel strength, like a renewal."

Tony continued with a guided visualization that helped Maggie to experience all the love that she had inside her and that she was ready to give, as well as all the strength that she was capable of.

I met with Maggie 2 years later, and she told me that, after this conversation with Tony, she was finally able to move past her son's death and had even become a prominent member of her community, devoting her time to charitable causes. When I asked her what was the most healing part of the experience with Tony, she said, "I was able to recover the memory of my son's sense of humor. I had forgotten that. And when I remembered, I realized how much he wanted me to be happy and fulfilled."

Joyous Joe

Joe was a hardworking entrepreneur who lived in California and loved his company. In 10 years he had built it from the ground up, and it was now worth $14 million. Not only that, the company made an enormous difference to Joe's community. It provided services for handicapped children and for the elderly. So the company was not just a source of income, it was a spiritual mission for Joe and his employees, who admired him and were like family to him. While he was developing the company, he went through a difficult divorce, but his mission sustained him.

Then suddenly there was a change in the state laws governing the services his company provided, and he was forced to close his business. At the same time, he lost most of what he had invested in a seemingly stable stock market fund, which was everything he owned other than the company. Even worse, at the request of a friend, he had invested her savings in the same failed fund, and she also lost her money.

Joe became deeply distraught and considered suicide. He took out a life insurance policy in the name of his friend and thought that if he killed himself, at least she would get the money from the insurance.

In a conversation with Tony Robbins, Joe realized that his most important values were responsibility and helping others. Money was not the most important thing.

By pointing this out, Tony showed he understood Joe. Then Tony got leverage by explaining to Joe that insurance doesn't pay in cases of suicide. He told Joe that if he died, Tony himself would send the videotape of their conversation to the insurance company. But most of all, Tony gained leverage by telling him the terrible suffering he would inflict on the friend whose money he had lost and who would feel forever guilty for his death.

Then Tony unexpectedly asked Joe to burp, and as Joe tried to do it, not very effectively, he laughed, and this changed his habitual pattern of grief and despair. Tony helped Joe realize that what he had to do was find work immediately and begin to pay back his friend for the money he had invested for her. In this way he defined the problem in solvable terms. But in order to come out of his despair, the work had to be meaningful. Joe soon after created a business that helps people who are in foreclosure to either save their home or find another one. Tony helped Joe to visualize all the happy moments from his past and to imagine all the joyful moments he would have in the future. He paid back his friend. On his calling card, his company is now called Joyous Joe.

Because we have all developed our own systems for regularly satisfying our needs, we tend to forget that we have made choices and developed habits. Often it is only through a crisis—a radical change—that we are able to realize that our choices and habits are provisional vehicles for meeting our needs and that we have many other alternatives that can be revised and expanded for long-term happiness. The secret for turning a crisis into an opportunity for growth is to recognize your pain as a growing pain, the kind of pain that is unavoidable but can be used to reassess your life, to strengthen and develop new ways of meeting your needs, so you can again experience happiness and take joy in the happiness of others.

We've all seen people who, while undergoing terribly painful and difficult circumstances, have been able to grow as human beings. We also know people who suddenly become "depressed" after overcoming a great struggle. When their crisis abates, these people seem to lose the impetus that was urging them to grow. They actually miss the crisis! Of course, it's not necessary to experience a crisis in order to grow. We all experience crises, but we have a choice in how we react to them.

Sometimes an individual will succumb to feelings of helplessness and misery and resort to drugs, alcohol, or another self-destructive behavior. Or he might become depressed, and almost revel in his depression, feeling it's what the world has inflicted upon him. When this occurs, all of his relationships are in jeopardy. What is it about depression that makes it easier to stay there than to change? Why is it that even when you are in mourning, in despair and misery, it feels comfortable, and impossible to crawl out of?

The Benefits of Sadness and Despair

An unfortunate aspect of human relationships is that sadness is a great connector. It brings people together much more easily than happiness. If you want to connect with someone, tell them your troubles, and the chances are that you will get sympathy and compassion. If, instead, you talk about your success and your happiness, chances are they'll find you boastful and will be less likely to connect with you.

People experience side benefits from holding on to "depression" and despair. These side benefits may offer temporary relief, but in the long term depression and despair are extremely destructive for everyone involved. To find the strength to overcome negative emotions, we must imagine a compelling future that will bring fulfillment and then move toward that future.

When you are in pain, you may have to work hard to see your options in life—to explore what is truly available to you, and then find a direction that will bring meaning and purpose back to your life.

Whatever your loss, the best cure for grief is to stop focusing on yourself and help others, be generous with your love, and focus on contribution.

No matter how devastating the loss, a compelling future is always available to you. As we have seen throughout this book, we all have beliefs and values that support simple steps toward growth, contribution, and life purpose. It is a matter of stopping panic, climbing out of despair, and finding what you value more than your pain and loss.

Steps for Creating a Compelling Future

1. Evaluate Your Initial Response.
2. Identify the Needs to Be Satisfied.
3. Understand the Side Benefits of Being in Despair.

4. Define Your True Purpose.

5. Find Multiple Ways to Achieve Your Purpose.

6. Use Your Body to Create Change in Yourself.

7. Create a Compelling Future.

Let's analyze these steps, one-by-one.

Step One: Evaluate Your Initial Response

When we experience a critical loss—losing someone or something that cuts to the core of our identity—we react, and often make a panicked, emergency attempt to reclaim what has been lost. Let's say your long-time lover leaves you. Suddenly, you focus on the needs he used to fulfill—and cast about frantically for some other way to fulfill those needs. There are two ways to react to such a crisis: a short-term "obtainable" reaction that will meet your immediate needs, and a longer-term "sustainable" reaction focused on making sure your needs are met in a positive way.

When you lose the primary person who has been meeting a basic need, you experience not only an emotional but also a physical loss. You may feel woozy, or get a sinking feeling in your stomach, or a pain in your heart. When you lose your sense of certainty and freedom, you may feel constricted or claustrophobic. When you lose your sense of significance and importance, you may feel small or unworthy. And when you lose love and connection, you feel shut out and alone. Because these experiences are so intense, people often reach out for the wrong kind of physical comfort—such as drugs, sex, alcohol, food, psychiatric medications—and even suicide as the ultimate solution to numb the pain.

A reaction is merely "obtainable" when its consequences will actually be negative to you and/or others in the future. A "sustainable" reaction, on the other hand, will continue to strengthen you over time. It can be a difficult decision to make in the midst of a devastating loss, especially since the obtainable action often seems easier, more immediate, within reach. When you react to a crisis or a radical change, the first question you should ask yourself is: Is this good for me *and* for others?

If you cannot honestly answer that your reaction is good both for you and for others, then you know you must abandon the obtainable reaction and find one that is sustainable. Instead of reaching for instant comfort, distraction, self-aggrandizement, or self-annihilation, ask yourself: What can I do now to provide for my needs and for others' needs in the future?

Step Two: Identify the Needs to Be Satisfied

Look back at Chapter 2. Which needs are you able to meet for yourself? Which are threatened by the loss you have sustained? It is in a crisis that our last two needs—for growth and contribution—can truly lift us out of despair.

To be in despair, you have to be focused on yourself and your own emotions. To come out of despair, you have to focus on others or on something outside of yourself so intensely that you don't have time to focus on your own emotions. That's why growth and contribution are the best ways to come out of despair. Growth may involve working on your art or learning something new. Contribution may be helping those who are in a worse situation than yourself or giving to a good cause.

Step Three: Understand the Side Benefits of Being in Despair

You probably have noticed how hard it is to communicate with someone who is in despair, overwhelmed by sadness, feeling helpless. You tend to walk on eggshells, worried that something you say or do will make them feel even worse; or even that they will misunderstand your concern and shut you out. In order to be able to communicate with someone who is despondent, we need to understand what that emotion does for them, just as we need to examine our own side benefits to being in despair. These side benefits may offer short-term relief, but over time they become destructive for everyone. Despair can make you feel cared for by others and released from your responsibilities. In the long term, however, despair is an imposition on the good will of others and will over time erode their sympathy, interest, and trust in you.

1. Despair reduces the sense of guilt because it feels like a form of penance.

2. Despair brings sympathy from others—and this sympathy can often feel like love.

3. Despair justifies abandoning relationships with family and friends with the idea that they will be better off without the desperate person.

4. Despair is an excuse for avoiding obligations and responsibilities.

5. Despair is a way of punishing others who feel they must help and yet fail to help.

6. Despair makes it difficult for significant others to leave because it would mean abandoning a desperate person.

7. Despair justifies indulging in addictions and other self-destructive, but momentarily pleasurable, behaviors.

8. Despair, especially when it comes together with the threat of suicide, is a way to dominate others who, afraid to upset the desperate person, will walk on eggshells.

There are two basic types of motivation behind despair: benign and hostile. Because despair is a cry for help, it can lead to benign feelings of connection and caring. But indulging in despair is also a way of imposing on others.

1. While despair gives a sense of doing penance, it is also a way to justify avoiding responsibility.

2. While despair brings sympathy, it is also a way of punishing others.

3. While despair justifies abandoning relationships, it also makes it difficult for people to leave the person in despair.

When you're in despair, you will typically focus on benign motivations and will fail to recognize the pain you're inflicting on others. The first step out of despair is to become aware of these side benefits and their consequences, and then to make a conscious decision not to indulge in despair.

Step Four: Define Your True Purpose

When we talk about our purpose, we are talking about something that gives greater meaning to our lives. You can define your purpose in terms of your values and the things you want to accomplish, but often it is best to define your purpose in terms of the needs that you wish to meet. The beauty of focusing on your needs is that you can always find a way to meet them, whatever the circumstances. Then the solution is sustainable over the long haul.

You can meet your need for certainty by knowing that you could buy a car or by knowing that you can afford to buy a book. The need for variety can be met by flying to Paris or by taking a walk. You can find significance by being appreciated by your children or by lecturing to 200 people. You can meet your need for love by being loved or by giving love. You can meet your need for growth by running a marathon or by reading a book. It is always your choice, and there always are ways of meeting your needs.

When you lose your habitual ways of meeting your needs, it is important to focus on what you truly feel gives your life meaning. Think about what has to happen for you to fulfill your top needs. What are your rules for satisfying your needs? In order to feel love and connection, do you need a full-time live-in partner, do you need a best friend or a circle of friends, or do you need a community of peers? In order to feel certainty, do you need a million dollars in the bank, do you need to have a steady job, or do you just need to know that you are capable of working? If you need significance, do you need others to treat you as important and accomplished, do you need the esteem of your family and friends, or do you need only to know that you have done your work well and helped others? Do your rules make it difficult or easy to succeed? Do your rules focus on things that are out of your control, or things that are in your control? Think about what needs you value most highly, and then think about what is truly required to fulfill your top needs. Make sure that the ways to fulfill your needs are within your control and consistent with your values.

Step Five: Find Multiple Ways to Achieve Your Purpose

Think about your main purpose in life. Is it to be happy, to be secure, or to be loved? Perhaps your main purpose is to make a contribution or to develop spiritually? Do you want to feel important, to be admired? Do you crave excitement and adventure? Whatever is your main purpose in life, there are many different ways to achieve it. Think of at least five different ways you could accomplish your purpose. Think of what could go wrong as you set about to accomplish that purpose. What could you do in times of difficulty that would ensure that you would meet your needs and enjoy success?

Step Six: Use Your Body to Create Change in Yourself

Defeat can become a pattern in your body—in fact, your body can become so accustomed to defeat that it can actually prevent you from recognizing opportunities for growth and happiness. You can assume a posture that empowers you—standing straight and energetic. You can do something silly or humorous to break the pattern of sadness. You can deliberately remember a time that makes you feel better and put your body in sync with that memory. Even a short burst of exercise will radically change the hormones in your body, your circulation, and your heart rate.

I know that shifting your posture doesn't solve the problem. But it is a way to enlist your physiology to help create an opportunity for change. There are times when the "talking cure" and introspection are not enough. If you are committed to taking a new direction in your life, it would be silly not to use your body to your advantage.

Go back to the time you experienced loss, and remember what it felt like—you may even feel your body tense up or deflate as you think back on that time. Identify where you are carrying the tension. What happens to your body as you think about that loss? Do you look up or down? Are you standing straight or hunched over? How are you holding your hands? Is your breathing fast, shallow, long, deep?

Now, make a change.

1. Stand up tall with your shoulders back.

2. Raise your arms above your head.

3. Jump or dance or shake your arms around.

4. Move in a way that gives you strength.

5. Do some push-ups, sit-ups, and jumping jacks.

6. Take 10 deep breaths.

7. Do something silly.

8. Throw a ball in the air.

9. Play with kids.

10. Read some jokes and laugh.

11. Take a bicycle ride or a long, invigorating walk.

Any one of these shifts not only will change your focus and your bio-chemistry but also will create an opportunity for you to recognize something new. It is true that our culture often does not support our changing our physiological states in a deliberate way. "Making a move" may seem simple. However, think of all the ways that we are changing our states all the time—by switching on the television, sitting down to relax, reading the newspaper, taking a walk, eating, having a drink. Everything on television is aimed at changing your state. The purpose of most music is to change your state. Take advantage of all the resources that are always available to you, including your body.

Step Seven: Create a Compelling Future

The process of creating a compelling future is crucial for putting your body, mind, and entire being in sync with the pursuit of your highest goals. In times of crisis, we almost always lose our feeling of certainty. When we have no certainty, it is difficult to experience deep emotion—it doesn't feel safe to feel. The process of creating a compelling future rebuilds certainty and helps you to fulfill all six of your needs.

Recall specific moments from your past when you were truly happy, times when you were having crazy fun, and recover your most joyous memories. Visualize those times, reach out, and pull them into your body. This helps engage your physiology and creates stronger ties to the memories of joy you are experiencing. Let them vibrate in your body. Feel this joy and exhilaration flood into your body.

Then step into the future. Imagine all the times yet to come when you will feel all of these emotions that you are currently experiencing and that you experienced in the past. Visualize these new memories that you will be experiencing in the future—how proud you will be, how connected, how grateful. Pull these new memories into your body. Enjoy the expectation of the memories that will come in the future.

Back from the Brink

I was asked by a business coach to consult with one of his clients who had told him he was planning to commit suicide. When Richard, an overweight, sad-looking man, walked into my office, I asked him how I could help him. He explained that he came from a poor, uneducated family and he had been the first one in the family to receive a college education. Success and hard work had always been central in his life. He had been laid off from work a year ago and was in such despair over not being able to find a job that he was considering suicide.

"You are going to have to explain this better to me because I don't understand it," I said. "You're saying you're going to kill yourself because you're not working? That's strange! Could you please explain?" *(Of course, I actually understood him very well—step one—but I was pretending not to understand him so I could help him evaluate his response to his loss.)*

He looked puzzled and replied, "Work is very important to a person's self-esteem. I feel worthless."

"You're going to have to explain that better," I said, continuing to play dumb. "I still don't get it."

He smiled a little, not sure whether I was joking.

"I'm serious," I said. "I'm quite a bit older than you—a child of the sixties. In my generation, nobody wanted to work. We were proud of not working. We wanted to tune in and drop out. So what's so great about work that you want to kill yourself because you don't have it?"

He was looking at me as if I had come from outer space. *(Step two—I was helping understand what needs were being met by his work.)*

He said, "I always thought that work was important. I have a strong work ethic."

"Hmm, what kind of work did you do?" I asked.

"I'm an engineer, and I always worked in plants manufacturing weapons."

"Oh, great," I said. "So the world is a better place because you're not working!" *(Step three—I was undercutting the side benefits of despair for him.)*

By now he was smiling broadly.

I said, "Look, eventually you'll go back to work—that's inevitable. And then you'll look back with regret on this period when you could have done so many things and had so much fun, because you won't have time any more to do the things you want to do. Do you have a girlfriend?" *(Step four—I identified his true purpose; step five—I was suggesting another way he might achieve his purpose, the possibility of having a girlfriend.)*

"No," he said. "I don't have any money."

"Since when is love related to money?" I asked. "If I were you, I would find a woman and go to the beach, the park, or the mountains. Go to the zoo." *(Step six—I was getting him to activate his physiology to energize himself.)*

Richard called me at my office the next day and said, "I just wanted to let you know that it's a beautiful day."

"Yes, it is," I agreed.

"And I'm at the zoo," he continued, and then he paused, "with a woman."

I said, "Great! And I'm at my office, working."

He wrote me a letter a year later to tell me that he was working and happy and to thank me for our conversation. (*Step seven—Richard had created a compelling future.*)

The story of my brief conversation with this man illustrates how easy it can be to create lasting change in situations that seem grim and hopeless. Most of the time, the barriers to our own well-being as well as to helping others, even with the most serious difficulties, are the beliefs and rules that limit our effectiveness.

Beyond Resolutions

In some relationships there are long-standing issues that will never be resolved, entrenched differences that may originate in family values, culture, gender, or personal preferences. If the relationship is to survive, those involved must understand and accept that the subject will probably never be resolved. The goal then becomes to keep an open, ongoing discussion in as mutually respectful and supportive a way as possible. Typical issues of this type are how much time should be devoted to home as opposed to work; whether the children should go to public school, private school, boarding school, or be homeschooled; what religion should be practiced; what constitutes religious practice; and so on. Rarely are these issues resolved. Sometimes a truce is reached for a while, and then an event triggers the issue again. Indirect negotiation is the best means by which to deal with irresolvable issues.

Steps for Indirect Negotiation

Step One: Clarify an Individual Question

Indirect negotiation operates on two levels, internally and interpersonally. Internally, the process begins with clarifying individual questions. The force that you would direct toward your partner is instead directed inward toward the clarification of your own values and emotional state. The negotiation must begin on the inside before it can be directed outward. Ask yourself specific questions about what you really want. The purpose of asking yourself these questions is to see your highest needs clearly. Because these needs are universal, they will be easier for your partner to understand than your point of view on the specific point you are debating.[2]

The questions you ask yourself must:

Be addressed to you.

Focus on your individual ability and sphere of control.

Direct you to take immediate representative action—to do something now that you believe in.

Take responsibility for all the meanings you construct. For example, instead of asking, "What are they doing to me?" ask, "What am I focusing on to make myself feel this way?"

Mention specific goals to achieve, using phrases like "How can I . . . " and "What can I do in order to . . . ?"

Uncover limiting assumptions in dealing with practical problems. For example, "What have I been focusing on that makes this problem seem unsolvable, and how can I get myself to a level where a solution appears?"

Target each individual's deepest wishes and the obstacles that block those wishes from coming true when the struggle is on how to proceed. For example, "What have I been focusing on that leads to conflict, what do I really want, and what can I do today to discover that?"[3]

In the example that follows, I use a married couple—Joe and Jenny—to show you how to use this technique, but you can also use it with a child, another relative, a friend, or when you want to help others solve a pernicious problem or at least to reach a truce.

First, Joe, in the presence of Jenny, defines the fundamental question. So Joe, after some hard thinking, will formulate his question along the lines of: "How can I love Jenny and encourage her love for me even though we don't see eye-to-eye as to how to raise our children?"

Step Two: Do Not Communicate Directly

Joe and Jenny cannot engage directly with one another until the process is complete—not with words, gestures, looks, or sounds. The purpose of blocking communication is to prevent Joe and Jenny from regarding each other as opponents and so quickly reaching a stalemate. By blocking direct communication, Joe and Jenny are forced to communicate indirectly, which helps each in their own internal negotiation to include the other's concerns. This puts Joe and Jenny into a state of "unconscious collaboration."

All the while Joe is doing this exercise, Jenny may not interrupt him, comment, or in any way react to anything Joe is saying. She can, however, take notes.

Step Three: Use a Meta-Frame and Negotiate Internally with Yourself

When Joe has formulated his question, he will then, still in Jenny's presence, ask the same question out loud of someone else, for instance, his father. So Joe will say, "Dad, how can I love Jenny and encourage her love for me even though we don't see eye-to-eye as to how to raise our children?" Then Joe will pretend to be his own father and will answer the question. Joe will repeat the question over and over to his imaginary father until he gets an enlightening answer.

Then he will ask the question of someone else, let's say his grandmother, and pretending to be his own grandmother he will answer the question as his grandmother would answer it, pressuring her in his imagination until the answer is enlightening. Then perhaps he will ask the question of a teacher or mentor. In this way a meta-frame is introduced so that the negotiation involves not just Joe and Jenny but also the father, the grandmother, and the mentor. All this time Jenny will be observing quietly, taking notes. Then it will be Jenny's turn, and she will formulate her question and answer it from the point of view of her father, her grandmother, and her mentor while Joe observes and takes notes.

Instead of using symbolic family members, you may want to use universal archetypes such as the Warrior, the Magician, the Lover, and the Sovereign or the Goddess. When we have a severe challenge and what we are doing is not working, chances are we will not solve the challenge with our usual resources. We need to find new resources. When you're struggling with a perceived injustice, have no idea what to do, or feel hurt or sad, it is useful to tap into other parts of yourself.

A variety of meta-frames can engage you with a number of points of view. When Jungian archetypes don't feel comfortable or appropriate, you can make up other labels. You can "name" your own archetype by asking yourself: When I feel powerful and engaged and can take on a challenge with my full energy, how do I think of myself? Find your own name for the Warrior—it might be Superman, the Can-Do Kid, or the Ubermom.

In engaging your archetypes, you can follow a sequence similar to that using the Jungian archetypes (the Warrior engages, the Magician makes it inventive, the Lover brings a sense of conscience, and the Sovereign consolidates into a vision). You can also use the meta-frame to take on specific people's perspectives, such as "What would Dad say?" and "What would Grandmother say?" Then you can answer, "Dad says to me . . . ," or "Grandmother says to me. . . ."

Whatever symbols you use in your negotiation, both of you will undergo an internal process that will make you more likely to feel empathy and understanding for each other. The process will help you develop wisdom and strength. Also, as you observe each other making the effort to resolve the issues within yourselves, you will feel more empathy and fellowship with each other. A tacit indirect agreement develops as each of you observes that the other is going through the same internal struggle. This indirect agreement then leads to direct agreement.

Step Four: Listen and Take Notes

Witnessing is an essential part of indirect negotiation. While Joe addresses the question to the imaginary archetypes or roles, Jenny observes and takes careful notes of everything that he says. This allows Jenny to listen nonjudgmentally and to truly absorb Joe's point of view.

Step Five: Indirect Agreement

When Joe is finished, Jenny repeats the same process with the same meta-frame that was chosen by Joe. As Jenny asks her question of the imaginary figures, and as she receives enlightened answers, an indirect agreement is reached. Joe and Jenny begin to realize that what they have in common is more important than their difference. The indirect agreement that develops when Joe and Jenny experience emotional parallels with each other is the basis of empathy and compassion.

Step Six: Direct Agreement

Direct agreement is reached spontaneously as both Joe and Jenny decide that they will not battle each other. At this point both have consolidated their emotional resources and have reached agreement on the most difficult elements in a negotiation: that they are truly equivalent, with the same needs, desires, and rights, and that both are deserving of protection, care, and representation.

////////////////////////////

It is important to understand that the meta-frame (be it archetypes, family figures, or some other configuration) works as a sequence, which is more than the sum of the individual images. Also, the process is solution oriented. It is used to seek answers to a specific question that will lead to specific decisions and behaviors. The entire process harnesses the force of emotion, turning it into a strength that will bring about unity.

CONCLUSION: BREAKING THROUGH TO GROWTH AND CONTRIBUTION

There are nine beliefs and patterns of behavior that restrict our possibilities for creating permanent loving bonds. These are what we have to watch out for:

1. The expectations that create problems: Be careful of what you expect from a relationship. Your expectation might become a self-fulfilling prophecy.

2. The theories we invent: Beware of the theories you invent to explain your relationships. Remember that we become attached to our theories no matter how inaccurate they might be.

3. The power of helplessness: Avoid resorting to helplessness as a source of power. It's not the kind of power that is conducive to a happy, permanent bond.

4. The plan for our relationships: Remember that if you don't plan your relationships, someone else will.

5. The emotions that rule: Practice experiencing the emotions that you enjoy experiencing instead of continuing to react to people or situations that upset you.

6. The beliefs that limit us: Don't poison yourself with negative beliefs about yourself and others.

7. The values that guide us: Establish as your highest values those that are consistent with happy, permanent bonds.

8. The responsibilities we avoid: Take responsibility for your relationships, and remember that you can change them to what you want them to be.

9. The blame we assign: Stop blaming everyone and everything else— your parents, your partner, your chemistry—for your problems. You have the power to choose to have the relationships you truly want.

What we choose to focus on determines how we feel. As you have seen, when we change our focus to love and connection, our problems can be solved. When we focus on our needs for love, for growth, and for contribution— on serving beyond ourselves—most emotional problems and sources of pain will disappear.

In many ways, contribution is the human need that effectively regulates your other five needs. If you are focused on contribution, you have the Certainty of being able to contribute (there is always a way), you have Variety (contribution is always interactive), you have Significance (the commitment to contribution defines you as a rare and extraordinary human being), you have Connection (helping others always creates a spiritual bond), and you have to Grow (to contribute requires going beyond your own needs).

THE BREAKTHROUGH ALPHABET

Here is an alphabet of key concepts we use to break through blocks in our relationships.

ARCHETYPES—WHEN you are in a conflict situation, negotiate with yourself first. Ask yourself what your Warrior, Magician, Lover, and Sovereign or Goddess would do. Think of what your child, your parent, your grandparent would advise. Appeal to your higher self before confronting the other person.

BELIEFS—TO develop our potential, we need to develop our beliefs. Our beliefs trigger our emotions, and our emotions lead us to action. Positive beliefs and expectations bring out the emotions that are necessary to develop and sustain happy relationships in every area of life. Make a list of your positive beliefs, and keep it where you can read it often. Cultivate the emotions that are triggered by these beliefs.

CONFLICT—EVERY conflict is a conflict between more than two people. Think about your current relationships at home, at work, with friends and relatives. Are you in conflict with someone? Who is the third party involved in your conflict? Could you resolve the conflict by changing the relationship with that third person?

DESPAIR—EXPERIENCING depression and despair has its benefits: It elicits sympathy, can be used as an excuse to avoid responsibilities, justifies indulging in addictions, punishes others, reduces guilt, justifies separations, and is used to dominate others. Be aware and acknowledge what depression and despair do to you and to others.

EMOTIONS—OUR emotions drive us: The heart controls the brain. Make a daily practice of experiencing positive emotions. Focus on feelings of love, compassion, joy, courage, determination, empathy, and these emotions will lead you toward a happier life. What are the positive emotions that you want to experience frequently? What beliefs would you have to develop in order to experience these emotions?

FUTURE—PRACTICE the process of creating a compelling future. Recover your joyous memories, visualize, reach out to them, and put them into your body. Feel flooded with joy and gratitude. Then step into the future. Imagine all the times yet to come where you will feel all of the joy that you are currently experiencing and will be experiencing in the future. Pull these new memories into your body. Enjoy the expectation of the memories that will come in the future.

GRATITUDE—FIND easy ways to experience gratitude on a daily basis. Research shows that gratitude is related to happiness. Experience gratitude for the simple things in life: your health, a good book, a beautiful day. Practice expressing gratitude to all those who have given to you and to those that you care for. It is important not just to experience gratitude but also to express it.

HELPLESSNESS—HELPLESSNESS is powerful. A person can develop a problem or an illness that makes them appear helpless yet empowers them to control and dominate others. A helpless spouse can dominate the marriage by organizing the behavior of the other spouse to compensate for the helplessness. Are you involved with a "personal-problem spouse"? Do you use helplessness to dominate? Be aware. When a person uses helplessness as a source of power, it is always because an underlying need is not being met.

INDIRECT COMMUNICATION—EVERY communication is both a direct and an indirect message. We often find ourselves ostensibly talking about one thing when we are really talking about something else. What indirect messages are you giving? Are they conducive to something positive? What indirect messages are you receiving? We are constantly influencing others and being influenced by others in indirect ways. A silence, a gesture, a tone of voice, a facial expression are communications that influence us constantly and with which we influence others.

JOY—FIND easy ways to experience joy on a daily basis. The sound of music, a walk in nature, a conversation with a friend, an act of kindness, a warm gesture—these are simple ways of experiencing the joy of living and enhancing the quality of your life.

KEY DECISIONS—FROM time to time it is useful to revisit key decisions that you made throughout your life, especially those made in early childhood. Are you burdened by key decisions that you made in the past and that are now obsolete? Make the effort to revisit these key decisions and change them.

LIFE CYCLE—THE way we want our needs to be met and what needs are most important to us change, depending on where we are in the life cycle. Younger people typically have a greater need for variety than older people. Those going through a critical time in their life usually have a greater need for certainty. Be sensitive to how your own needs change and also to the changes in the needs of those around you. How have your partner's needs changed over time? Do you know?

MALIGNANT ESCALATION—TOO much equality can lead to malignant escalation. Do you have such an egalitarian relationship with your partner that you must decide everything together? Do you find yourself competing with your partner as to who is right, more competent, or a better person? Think about how you can divide areas of expertise and so avoid conflicts.

NEEDS—TO win and to keep someone's love, you must satisfy their six human needs: certainty, variety, significance, love, growth, and contribution. If you satisfy two of these needs, you have established a relationship. If you satisfy four of these needs, you have developed a deep bond. If you satisfy all six human needs for someone, he or she will be permanently bonded to you. Are you satisfying the six human needs for your partner, your loved ones?

ORGANIZATIONS—OUR lives are organized in hierarchies, and hierarchies can lead to dangerous cross-generational coalitions. Do you side with a child against your spouse? Do you sometimes take your mother's side against your husband? Are you in a coalition with a colleague against a supervisor or a boss? Take some time to reflect on the cross-generational coalitions in your life. How do you benefit from them? How do they give you pain? How can you break them?

PATTERNS—WE relate in patterns that repeat. Do you find yourself having the same discussion over and over again? What negative repetitive sequences are you involved in, and with whom? How can you break these patterns?

QUESTIONS—THE quality of your life depends on the questions you ask yourself on a regular basis. A person who asks, "What are my limitations?" will have a very different life from one who asks, "What are my strengths?" Develop quality questions, and the answers will lead you to better relationships. Focus on creating a primary question of the highest possible level of growth and contribution.

RESPONSIBILITY—YOU are responsible for your own life and for the well-being of those you love. If you are unhappy, take responsibility for finding easier ways to satisfy your six human needs. If your partner, your children, or your parents are unhappy, find ways to satisfy their six human needs. Take responsibility for how you contribute to the emotions of others.

SELF-DETERMINATION—YOU can't blame your parents, your teachers, your traumas, or the state of the world. Even under the most dire circumstances, there is a choice to be made. You have the power to determine who you are and who you're going to be.

TRIANGLES—RELATIONSHIPS are organized in triangles. Even though we love to be in a twosome, twosomes quickly become triangles. What triangles are you involved in? How can you create a boundary around a twosome? Can you protect your relationship with your spouse from intrusions by the children? Can you protect your relationship with a child from intrusions by your spouse? What are the positive triangles in your life? What triangles would you prefer not to be involved in? We can escape triangles by being part of circles—that is, relationships among equals, like a circle of friends.

UNDERLYING VALUES—THE more serious the conflict, the more it is about underlying values. Think of a conflict that you are currently involved in or one that you've had in the past. What were your underlying values? What values did the other person hold? Could you adjust your values and resolve the conflict? What values do you and your partner share? What values do you disagree on? Could you adjust your values for the sake of greater harmony?

VEHICLES—VEHICLES are the means by which you satisfy your needs. Everyone has the same six human needs, but the means by which these needs are satisfied, the vehicles, vary from person to person. Someone may only experience certainty, for example, if they have a million dollars in the bank. Someone else may experience certainty simply by having a job. We can't change the fact that we all have the same human needs, but we can change the vehicles by which those needs are satisfied and so make life easier and happier for ourselves.

WASTE—EVERY moment of your life is precious. Don't waste it. Stay focused on love, growth, and contribution. Your life will never be wasted if you focus on satisfying the six human needs of those you love.

"XEMPLARY"—THE way you live is an example for those around you and for future generations. If you live with love and passion, with growth and contribution, or with resentment and fear, you are giving an example to others, and you are contributing to others' living in the same way.

YOU—ARE in charge of your life and your relationships, and you can use the tools in this book to break through blocks and create the fabulous, fulfilling relationships you want.

ZERO IN—FOCUS on what is most important to you, to those you love, to your community, and to the world.

The Workbook

The exercises that follow are meant to be used when you are ready to make a change in your life and your relationships. You can complete these exercises alone, or better, with the person with whom you want to solve a conflict. It's very interesting to compare results with the other person.

Is the person surprised by some of the ways you've answered the questions? If so, why? Are you surprised by some of their answers? If you express surprise, and push them to further explain their answers, do they become defensive? Do you? When you push, where do they go? Where do you go? This is always a clue to what's really going on.

//

What is the source of the conflict?

Define the problem in concrete terms:

_____

_____

_____

_____

_____

Have your partner define it in concrete terms:

_____

_____

_____

_____

_____

_____

What are you focusing on?

_____

_____

_____

_____

_____

What is your partner focusing on?

_____

_____

_____

_____

_____

What does your body feel like when you experience this problem?

_____

_____

_____

_____

What does your partner's body feel like when she/he experiences this problem?

_____

_____

_____

_____

_____

_____

What meaning do you give to it?

_____

_____

_____

_____

_____

What meaning does he/she give to it?

_____

_____

_____

_____

_____

_____

It is interesting to see how two parties in a conflict might define the problem differently. That's the first step to finding a solution.

Make a list of behaviors that you would like to change. Next to each one, write how you have been attempting to change this behavior. Then write a totally different solution.

BEHAVIOR 1: _____

_____

_____

Previous attempt to change: _____

_____

_____

_____

_____

New solution:_____

_____

_____

_____

BEHAVIOR 2:_____

_____

_____

Previous attempt to change:_____

_____

_____

_____

New solution:_____

_____

_____

_____

BEHAVIOR 3:_____

_____

_____

Previous attempt to change: _____

_____

_____

_____

New solution: _____

_____

_____

//

Now ask your partner (child, sibling, parent, etc.) to do the same.

BEHAVIOR 1: _____

_____

Previous attempt to change: _____

_____

_____

_____

New solution: _____

_____

_____

BEHAVIOR 2: _____

_____

Previous attempt to change: _____

_____

_____

New solution: _____

_____

_____

BEHAVIOR 3: _____

_____

Previous attempt to change: _____

_____

_____

New solution: _____

_____

_____

What are your needs?

Here are the six human needs:

Certainty   Love/Connection

Uncertainty/Variety   Growth

Significance   Contribution

Now list them in the order that they are important to you, the first being the most important:

1. _____

2. _____

3. _____

4. _____

5. _____

6. _____

Which are your two most important needs? How do they determine the course of your life?

NEED 1: _____

_____

_____

How does it determine the course of my life?_____

_____

_____

_____

NEED 2:_____

_____

How does it determine the course of my life?_____

_____

_____

_____

//

Now ask your partner to do the same.

NEED 1: _____

_____

How does it determine the course of my life?_____

_____

_____

NEED 2: _____

_____

How does it determine the course of my life?_____

_____

_____

_____

_____

Is either of you surprised by the other's list?

///

Think about it.

Do you value certainty over love/connection? Do you value uncertainty/variety over significance? What if your driving force were growth? How would that be different from valuing significance over anything else? There are no right or wrong answers. Discuss the six human needs with your partner (child, sibling, parent). Explain what you value. Listen to him or her. Discover what you need to know to have a better relationship and to make each other happy.

Next, think of your top two needs. What would change in your life if one of them changed? Are you ready to change which needs you value most? Your happiness might depend on your flexibility to change which needs are most important to you.

My new two most important needs:

NEED 1: _____

_____

How does it determine the course of my life?_____

_____

_____

_____

_____

_____

NEED 2: _____

_____

How does it determine the course of my life?_____

_____

_____

_____

_____

_____

Ask your partner to do the same.

///

My partner's new two most important needs:

NEED 1: _____

_____

How does it determine the course of my life?_____

_____

_____

_____

_____

NEED 2: _____

_____

How does it determine the course of my life?_____

_____

_____

_____

_____

YOUR RELATIONSHIP

Now imagine you are your partner, and from his/her perspective, rate how successfully you have been meeting your partner's needs in the past.

I have been meeting my partner's needs from his/her perspective:

Certainty

From your partner's perspective, how well have you been meeting his/her need for certainty? _____

Your Score (1 to 10, with 10 being the highest) _____

Why?_____

_____

_____

_____

Name three ways you could meet this need for your partner:

1. _____

2. _____

3. _____

Uncertainty/Variety

How well have you been meeting his/her need for uncertainty/ variety? _____

Your Score _____

Why? _____

_____

_____

Name three ways you could meet this need for your partner:

1 _____

2. _____

3. _____

Significance

How well have you been meeting her/his need for significance?

_____

Your Score_____

Why?_____

_____

_____

_____

Name three ways you could meet this need for your partner:

1. _____

2. _____

3. _____

//

Love/Connection

How well have you been meeting his/her need for love/connection?

_____

Your Score_____

Why?_____

_____

_____

_____

Name three ways you could meet this need for your partner:

1. _____

2. _____

3. _____

///

Growth

How well have you been meeting her/his need for growth?

_____

Your Score_____

Why?_____

_____

_____

_____

Name three ways you could meet this need for your partner:

1. _____

2. _____

3. _____

Contribution

How well have you been meeting his/her need for Contribution?

_____

Your Score_____

Why?_____

_____

_____

_____

Name three ways you could meet this need for your partner:

1. _____

2. _____

3. _____

Now rate yourself from your own perspective. How well have you been meeting your partner's needs?

I have been meeting my partner's needs from my own perspective:

Certainty

How well have you been meeting his/her need for certainty?

_____

Your Score_____

Why?_____

_____

_____

_____

Name three ways you could meet this need for your partner:

1. _____

2. _____

3. _____

Uncertainty/Variety

How well have you been meeting his/her need for uncertainty/ variety? _____

Your Score_____

Why?_____

_____

_____

Name three ways you could meet this need for your partner:

1. _____

2. _____

3. _____

Significance

How well have you been meeting her/his need for significance?

_____

Your Score_____

Why?_____

_____

_____

_____

Name three ways you could meet this need for your partner:

1. _____

2. _____

3. _____

//

Love/Connection

How well have you been meeting her/his need for love/connection?

_____

Your Score_____

Why?_____

_____

_____

_____

Name three ways you could meet this need for your partner:

1. _____

2. _____

3. _____

//

Growth

How well have you been meeting his/her need for growth?

_____

Your Score_____

Why?_____

_____

_____

_____

Name three ways you could meet this need for your partner:

1. _____

2. _____

3. _____

Contribution

How well have you been meeting her/his need for contribution?

_____

Your Score_____

Why?_____

_____

_____

Name three ways you could meet this need for your partner:

1. _____

2. _____

3. _____

Now repeat the same exercise, and rate how well you think your partner has been meeting your six needs.

My partner has been meeting my six needs from my own perspective:

Certainty

My partner has been meeting my need for certainty:

His/Her Score_____

Why?_____

_____

_____

Name three ways your partner could meet your need for certainty:

1. _____

2. _____

3. _____

//

Uncertainty/Variety

My partner has been meeting my need for uncertainty/variety:

Her/His Score_____

Why?_____

_____

_____

Name three ways your partner could meet your need for uncertainty/variety:

1. _____

2. _____

3. _____

//

Significance

My partner has been meeting my need for significance:

His/Her Score_____

Why?_____

_____

_____

Name three ways your partner could meet your need for significance:

1. _____

2. _____

3. _____

Love/Connection

My partner has been meeting my need for love/connection:

Her/His Score_____

Why?_____

_____

_____ .

Name three ways your partner could meet your need for love/
connection:

1. _____

2. _____

3. _____

Growth

My partner has been meeting my need for growth:

Her/His Score_____

Why?_____

_____

_____

Name three ways your partner could meet your need for growth:

1. _____

2. _____

3. _____

//

Contribution

My partner has been meeting my need for contribution:

His/Her Score_____

Why?_____

_____

Name three ways your partner could meet your need for contribution:

1. _____

2. _____

3. _____

//

Now ask your partner how he/she thinks he/she has been meeting your needs from his/her perspective.

//

My partner thinks he/she has been meeting my needs from his/her perspective:

//

Certainty

My partner thinks he/she has been meeting my need for certainty from his/her perspective:

My partner scores him/herself _____

Why? _____

_____

_____

My partner names three ways he/she could meet my need for certainty:

1. _____

2. _____

3. _____

Uncertainty/Variety

My partner thinks she/he has been meeting my need for uncertainty/variety from her/his perspective:

My partner scores her/himself _____

Why?_____

_____

_____

My partner names three ways she/he could meet my need for uncertainty/variety:

1. _____

2. _____

3. _____

Significance

My partner thinks he/she has been meeting my need for significance from his/her perspective:

My partner scores him/herself_____

Why?_____

_____

_____

My partner names three ways he/she could meet my need for significance:

1. _____

2. _____

3. _____

//

Love/Connection

My partner thinks she/he has been meeting my need for love/connection from her/his perspective:

My partner scores her/himself_____

Why?_____

_____

_____

My partner names three ways she/he could meet my need for love/
connection:

1. _____

2. _____

3. _____

///

Growth

My partner thinks he/she has been meeting my need for growth
from his/her perspective:

My partner scores him/herself_____

Why?_____

_____

_____

My partner names three ways he/she could meet my need for
growth:

1. _____

2. _____

3. _____

Contribution

My partner thinks she/he has been meeting my need for contribution from her/his perspective:

My partner scores her/himself _____

Why?_____

_____

_____

My partner names three ways she/he could meet my need for contribution:

1. _____

2. _____

3. _____

Take the time to share your answers with each other and to make sure that each understands the other's needs and point of view.

What are the vehicles by which you satisfy your needs?

It is important to differentiate between your needs and vehicles—the actions, beliefs, and behaviors you use to meet your needs. For example, you might believe that for you to feel loved, your spouse must hug you every day. Your belief is that if you are not hugged, you are not loved. The hug is your vehicle to satisfy your need to be loved. It is a belief about what has to happen to have your need for love met. Many people think that what they want most is wealth and material possessions, but these are just vehicles for satisfying their need for significance or perhaps for certainty.

Write each of the six human needs in the spaces below in the same order in which you placed them earlier (so that Need #1 is your greatest need). Then think about three different ways by which you currently satisfy each need. Write these three vehicles in the numbered list for each need.

NEED 1: _____

_____

I currently satisfy this need by:

1. _____

2. _____

3. _____

NEED 2: _____

_____

I currently satisfy this need by:

1. _____

2. _____

3. _____

NEED 3: _____

_____

I currently satisfy this need by:

1. _____

2. _____

3. _____

NEED 4: _____

_____

I currently satisfy this need by:

1. _____

2. _____

3. _____

NEED 5: _____

_____

I currently satisfy this need by:

1. _____

2. _____

3. _____

NEED 6: _____

I currently satisfy this need by:

1. _____

2. _____

3. _____

//

Ask your partner to do the same:

NEED 1: _____

_____

I currently satisfy this need by:

1. _____

2. _____

3. _____

NEED 2: _____

_____

I currently satisfy this need by:

1. _____

2. _____

3. _____

NEED 3: _____

_____

I currently satisfy this need by:

1. _____

2. _____

3. _____

NEED 4: _____

_____

I currently satisfy this need by:

1. _____

2. _____

3. _____

NEED 5: _____

_____

I currently satisfy this need by:

1. _____

2. _____

3. _____

NEED 6: _____

_____

I currently satisfy this need by:

1. _____

2. _____

3. _____

What insights have you gained about how you fulfill your needs?
What changes could you make that would allow your partner to
fulfill your needs?

What insights have you gained about what your partner needs and about what you could do to fulfill more of his or her needs?

Ask your partner how she or he would like to have needs met. Discover your partner's preferences. What has to happen for your partner to feel that the top three needs are being met? *Be specific.* The more specific you are, the easier it will be to discover the triggers that will allow you to satisfy your partner's needs, thereby deepening your connection.

Share what you would appreciate receiving from your partner. Be aware that your partner may interpret this as a trade-off. "Since I gave you yours, now you owe me mine." If this is a concern, make a point of giving to your partner for a period of time without expecting anything back. This should restore good faith, encouraging your partner to be more responsive. Make sure to phrase your needs with humility and respect. Share your list with your partner and brainstorm ways of meeting each of your needs.

///

Your Model of the World

Key Decisions: Look back at Chapter 6. What key decisions have you made? What key decisions has your partner made? Ask each other: What key decisions do you think I've made?

Values: Quickly and spontaneously as it comes to mind, make a list (on the next page) of everything you value—list as many values as you can think of in a few minutes.

Your list might include, for example, adventure, fun, love, contribution, lifestyle, integrity, harmony, health, family, friends, empathy, compassion, fairness, humility, courage, humor, security, personal development, political leadership, and creativity. These are just some of the words that refer to common values. You probably have your own words.

_____

_____

_____

_____

_____

Now ask your partner to list her/his values as the words come to mind:

_____

_____

_____

_____

_____

Now pick the first 10 values on your list and write them down in order of importance, from the most important to the least:

1. _____

2. _____

3. _____

4. _____

5. _____

6. _____

7. _____

8. _____

9. _____

10. _____

Ask your partner to pick the first 10 values on his/her list and write them down in order of importance, from the most important to the least:

1. _____

2. _____

3. _____

4. _____

5. _____

6. _____

7. _____

8. _____

9. _____

10. _____

Now examine your list and think about whether these values and the order in which they are listed truly reflect what you value most in your life today. Many of us continue to live by values that we developed when we were younger, which may be obsolete in the present. For example, someone might continue to put adventure and fun at the top of their list, when in their current situation they should place a higher value on health or family. Now, after careful consideration, rewrite the order of importance of your values, to reflect more accurately how you want to live today:

1. _____

2. _____

3. _____

4. _____

5. _____

6. _____

7. _____

8. _____

9. _____

10. _____

Now ask your partner to reconsider her/his list and to rewrite the order of importance of her/his values to reflect more accurately how she/he wants to live today:

1. _____

2. _____

3. _____

4. _____

5. _____

6. _____

7. _____

8. _____

9. _____

10. _____

For each of your top three values, list three ways that you can experience that value every day or every week. Try to find easy ways to fulfill the value. What are three ways that every day or every week you can experience adventure, fun, love, making a contribution—whatever is on your list?

VALUE 1: _____

I can fulfill this value on a regular basis by:

1. _____

2. _____

3. _____

VALUE 2: _____

I can fulfill this value on a regular basis by:

1. _____

2. _____

3. _____

VALUE 3: _____

I can fulfill this value on a regular basis by:

1. _____

2. _____

3. _____

///

Now ask your partner, for each of his/her top three values, to list three ways in which he/she could experience that value every day or every week:

VALUE 1: _____

I can fulfill this value on a regular basis by:

1. _____

2. _____

3. _____

VALUE 2: _____

I can fulfill this value on a regular basis by:

1. _____

2. _____

3. _____

VALUE 3: _____

I can fulfill this value on a regular basis by:

1. _____

2. _____

3. _____

Compare your values and the ways you fulfill them with those of your partner. If they are similar, the chances are that the relationship is stable. Differences are an indication of conflict. But once a conflict has been identified, it can be solved. You can begin to understand and accept your differences, or you can work to reconcile your values and means of fulfilling them.

It's a good practice to review your list of values every year and change them to reflect your current situation and what you truly want now.

///

References: Who are your most influential life models? (for example, parents, teachers, family members, friends, colleagues, mentors)

1. _____

2. _____

3. _____

Could you choose better life models? Who would they be?

1. _____

2. _____

3. _____

///

Habitual Questions: What are the habitual questions you ask yourself? (For example, do you ask yourself, "How could I make this better?" Or do you ask yourself, "Why don't I do anything right?")

1. _____

2. _____

3. _____

What questions could you ask yourself that would lead to a better quality of life for you and for those you love?

1. _____

2. _____

3. _____

//

Emotions: Make a list of all the emotions you experience in any given week or month.

_____

_____

_____

_____

_____

_____

_____

_____

_____

_____

Now list these emotions in the order of the ones you experience most frequently (you will probably find that there are only three or four emotions that you experience on a regular basis):

_____

_____

_____

_____

_____

Now, of these emotions, list those that are most intense:

_____

_____

_____

Are these the emotions you want to experience?_____

What emotions would you prefer? Write them down:

_____

_____

_____

_____

_____

Ask your partner to do the same, then compare. Once again, see if your partner is surprised by your list, or vice versa.

We know how easily our emotions can change. Everyone has had the experience, for example, of feeling sad, and then someone tells you a joke and you're laughing. You instantly changed from sadness to joy. If this can happen to you once, it can happen always. You can deliberately choose what emotions you want to experience most frequently.

Now, for each emotion that you would prefer to experience, write three ways you can ensure that you will experience that emotion on a daily basis:

EMOTION 1: _____

I will experience this emotion on a daily basis by doing or thinking the following:

1. _____

2. _____

3. _____

EMOTION 2: _____

I will experience this emotion on a daily basis by doing or thinking the following:

1. _____

2. _____

3. _____

EMOTION 3: _____

I will experience this emotion on a daily basis by doing or thinking the following:

1. _____

2. _____

3. _____

//

At what stage are you in your relationship?

//

Stages of the Life Cycle

    The Courtship Period

    Early Marriage

    Childbirth and Dealing with the Young

    Middle Marriage

    Weaning Parents from Children

    Retirement and Old Age

What stages have you already gone through?

_____

_____

_____

_____

_____

_____

What changes do you have to make to adapt and successfully
navigate through the current stage?

_____

_____

_____

_____

_____

What help can you expect from others?

_____

_____

_____

_____

_____

What adjustments can you make in your relationship, taking into consideration the life cycle rather than individual traits and desires?

_____

_____

_____

///

Do you have a plan from day to day, or in broad life terms?

Whose plan are you following?

_____

_____

Whenever you feel someone is pushing your buttons, it's time to reflect that perhaps you are following someone else's plan—and you may not even be aware of it.

_____

_____

_____

Are you and your loved ones following the same plan, or different ones?

_____

_____

What are the repeating sequences of interaction in your relationship?

What weapons do you habitually use? (These can include humor, sarcasm, criticism, teasing, threats, anger, silence, mocking gestures, violence, and so forth.)

List the weapons you commonly use:

1. _____

2. _____

3. _____

4. _____

5. _____

Do you and your partner agree on what weapons each other uses?

_____

_____

Are you communicating through metaphor?

_____

Could a challenge you are facing be a metaphor for a more important problem?

_____

_____

Do you know how to communicate affection in the way your partner prefers?

Is it through special words, touch, gifts?

_____

_____

Find out your partner's true preferences.

_____

_____

The System

How are your extended family, friends, co-workers involved in your relationship?

_____

_____

What triangles are you involved in? Are they helpful or destructive?

_____

_____

Are you involved in cross-generational coalitions? Are they detrimental? If so, who are they hurting?

_____

_____

What hierarchies inform the relationship?

_____

_____

_____

Who has the power over various areas in the relationship?

_____

_____

Make a list; ask your partner to do the same.

Areas of control:

1. _____

2. _____

3. _____

4. _____

5. _____

Do you and your partner agree with each other's lists?

_____

_____

What areas do you wish you had control over?

_____

_____

///

HOW TO BREAK THROUGH

Now that you know your needs, your model of the world, and the shape of your relationship, you can see clearly what changes need to be made.

1. Change your focus to your needs for love, growth, and contribution.

2. Lay down your weapons.

3. Change your expectations.

4. Change your habitual response—break the pattern—be outrageous.

5. Change your physiology.

6. Call on the archetypes (in any form they work for you) to discover what you truly want.

7. Call on your networks for support.

END NOTES

———— //////////////////////////// ————

Chapter 1

1. Schneiria, T.C., and G. Piel. "The Army Ant." *Twentieth-Century Bestiary*. By the editors of *Scientific American*. New York: Simon & Schuster, 1955.

2. Watzlawick, P. " 'Insight' May Cause Blindness." *The Evolution of Psychotherapy—The Third Conference*. Ed. J. Zeig. New York: Brunner/Mazel Publishers, 1995.

3. Madanes, C. *Sex, Love, and Violence—Strategies for Transformation*. New York: Norton, 1990.

4. Thomas, L. *The Medusa and the Snail*. New York: Bantam Books, 1980.

5. Lewis Thomas (1980).

Chapter 2

1. Maslow in his 1943 paper, "A Theory of Human Motivation," proposed a hierarchy of needs that are usually depicted as a pyramid going from the most basic level of Physiological Needs to Safety, Love/Belonging, Esteem, and Self-Actualization. John A.

215

Schindler M.D. (*How to Live 365 Days a Year,* Prentice-Hall, 1954) proposed that there are six basic human needs: Love, Security, Creative Expression, Recognition, New Experiences ,and Self-Esteem.

2. Robbins, A., and C. Madanes. *Back from the Edge.* A film from the Robbins-Madanes Center for Strategic Intervention, 2005.

3. Haley, J. Uncommon Therapy: The Psychiatric Techniques of Milton H. Erickson. New York: Norton, 1973.

4. Adizes, I. Managing Corporate Lifecycles. Upper Saddle River, NJ: Prentice-Hall Press, 1999.

Chapter 3

1. The Bavelas' experiment is discussed in Watzlawick, Paul, 1976.

2. Watzlawick, P. How Real Is Real? Confusion, Disinformation, Communication. New York: Norton, 1976.

3. Damasio, A. R. Descartes' Error: Emotion, Reason and the Human Brain. New York: Avon Books, 1995.

4. Le Doux, J. The Emotional Brain: The Mysterious Underpinnings of Emotional Life. New York: Touchstone Books, 1998.

5. Zweig, J. "Are You Wired for Wealth?" Money, October 2002.

6. Schultz, W. "Getting Formal with Dopamine and Reward." Neuron 36 (2002): 241–63.

7. Zweig, J. "Are You Wired for Wealth?" Money, October 2002.

8. Keim, C. Personal communication. 2003.

9. Siegel, Daniel. The Developing Mind: How Relationships and the Brain Interact to Shape Who We Are. New York: Guilford Press, 1999.

10. Siegel, Daniel. The Developing Mind: How Relationships and the Brain Interact to Shape Who We Are. New York: Guilford Press, 1999.

Chapter 4

1. Volk, T. Metapatterns—Across Space, Time, and Mind. New York: Columbia University Press, 1995.

2. Bennis, W. "The End of Leadership: Exemplary Leadership Is Impossible without Full Inclusion, Initiatives, and Cooperation of Followers." *Organizational Dynamics* 28, no. 1 (Summer 1999): 71–79.

3. Caplow, T. *Two Against One—Coalitions in Triads.* Upper Saddle River, NJ: Prentice-Hall, 1968.

4. Madanes, C. *The Secret Meaning of Money.* San Francisco: Jossey-Bass, 1994.

5. Bateson, G. *Steps to an Ecology of Mind.* New York: Ballantine Books, 1972. Reprinted with a foreword by Mary Catherine Bateson. Chicago: University of Chicago Press, 2000.

6. Madanes, C. *The Therapist As Humanist, Social Activist and Systemic Thinker . . . And Other Selected Papers.* Phoenix, AZ: Zeig, Tucker, and Theisen, 2006.

Chapter 5

1. Lacan, J. *The Four Fundamental Concepts of Psycho-Analysis.* New York: W.W. Norton & Company, 1981.

2. Bateson, G., and D. D. Jackson. "Some Varieties of Pathogenic Organization." In *Communication, Family and Marriage.* Vol. 1. Ed. D. D. Jackson. Palo Alto, CA: Science and Behavior Books, 1968.

3. Madanes, C. *Strategic Family Therapy.* San Francisco: Jossey-Bass, 1981.

4. Madanes, C. *Sex, Love, and Violence—Strategies for Transformation.* New York: Norton, 1990.

5. Seligman (1990).

6. Laing, R. D. *The Politics of the Family and Other Essays.* New York: Pantheon Books, 1969.

7. Laing, R. D. *The Politics of the Family and Other Essays.* New York: Pantheon Books, 1969.

8. Rosenthal, R., and L. Jacobson. *Pygmalion in the Classroom.* Expanded edition. New York: Irvington, 1992.

9. Rosenthal, R. *Judgment Studies: Design, Analysis, and Meta-Analysis.* New York: Cambridge University Press, 1987.

10. Halverson, A. M., M. Hallahan, A. J. Hart, and R. Rosenthal. "Reducing the Biasing Effects of Judges' Nonverbal Behavior with Simplified Jury Instruction." *Journal of Applied Psychology* 82 (1997): 590–98.

Chapter 6

1. Robbins, A., and C. Madanes. *Reclaiming Your True Identity: The Power of Vulnerability.* A film from the Robbins-Madanes Center for Strategic Intervention, 2004.

2. For more details and advice for cases of serious abuse, see Madanes, C. *Sex, Love and Violence*, Norton, 1990 and *The Violence of Men*, Jossey-Bass, 1995.

Chapter 7

1. For more about Milton Erikson and his work, see Haley, Jay, ed. *Advanced Techniques of Hypnosis and Therapy—Selected Papers of Milton H. Erickson, M.D.* New York: Grune & Stratton, 1967.

2. Bandler, Richard, and John Grinder. *Patterns of the Hypnotic Techniques of Milton H. Erickson, M.D.* Vol. 1. Cupertino, CA: Meta Publications, 1975.

3. Grinder, J., J. DeLozier, and R. Bandler. *Patterns of the Hypnotic Techniques of Milton H. Erickson, M.D.* Vol. 2. Cupertino, CA: Meta Publications, 1977.

Chapter 8

1. Seligman, Martin. *Learned Optimism.* New York: Alfred A. Knopf, Inc., 1990.

2. Jung, C. G. *Portable Jung.* New York: Viking Penguin Inc., 1971.

3. Madanes, C. *Strategic Family Therapy.* San Francisco: Jossey-Bass, 1981.

4. Ricardo Chouhy, Ph.D. was the therapist in this case

Chapter 9

1. Robbins, A., and C. Madanes. *Conquering Overwhelming Loss: Rediscovering a Compelling Future.* A film from the Robbins-Madanes Center for Strategic Intervention, 2004, and the accompanying Pejcha, M., and C. Madanes, *Action Book* for the film *Conquering Overwhelming Loss: Rediscovering a Compelling Future.* La Jolla, CA: Robbins-Madanes Center for Strategic Intervention, 2004.

2. Robbins, A., and C. Madanes. *Negotiating Conflict: Leadership in Times of Crisis.* A film from the Robbins-Madanes Center for Strategic Intervention, 2004, and the accompanying Pejcha, M., and C. Madanes, *Action Book* for the film *Negotiating Conflict: Leadership in Times of Crisis.* La Jolla, CA: Robbins-Madanes Center for Strategic Intervention, 2004.

3. Robbins, A., and C. Madanes. *Negotiating Conflict: Leadership in Times of Crisis.* A film from the Robbins-Madanes Center for

Strategic Intervention, 2004, and the accompanying Pejcha, M., and C. Madanes, *Action Book* for the film *Negotiating Conflict: Leadership in Times of Crisis*. La Jolla, CA: Robbins-Madanes Center for Strategic Intervention, 2004.

BIBLIOGRAPHY

―――― *//////////////////////////* ――――

Adizes, Ichak. *Managing Corporate Lifecycles.* New York: Prentice Hall Press, 1999.

Bandler, Richard, and John Grinder. *Patterns of the Hypnotic Techniques of Milton H. Erickson, M.D.* Vol. 1. Cupertino, CA: Meta Publications, 1975.

Bateson, Gregory. *Steps to an Ecology of Mind.* New York: Ballantine Books, 1972. Reprinted with a foreword by Mary Catherine Bateson. Chicago: University of Chicago Press, 2000.

―――――. *Mind and Nature, A Necessary Unity.* New York: E.P. Dutton, 1979.

Bateson, Gregory, and Don D. Jackson. "Some Varieties of Pathogenic Organization." In *Communication, Family and Marriage.* Vol. 1. Ed. Don D. Jackson. Palo Alto, CA: Science and Behavior Books, 1968.

Bennis, Warren. "The End of Leadership: Exemplary Leadership Is Impossible without Full Inclusion, Initiatives, and Cooperation of Followers." *Organizational Dynamics* 28, no. 1 (Summer 1999): 71-79.

Caplow, Theodore. *Two Against One—Coalitions in Triads.* Englewood Cliffs, New Jersey: Prentice-Hall, 1968.

Damasio, Antonio R. *Descartes' Error: Emotion, Reason, and the Human Brain*. New York: Avon Books, 1995.

Frankl, Viktor. *Man's Search for Meaning*. Boston: Beacon Press, 1959.

Gottman, John. Personal communication. 2004.

Grinder, John, Judith DeLozier, and Richard Bandler. *Patterns of the Hypnotic Techniques of Milton H. Erickson, M.D.* Vol. 2. Cupertino, CA: Meta Publications, 1977.

Haley, Jay. *Uncommon Therapy: The Psychiatric Techniques of Milton H. Erickson, M.D.* New York: Norton, 1973.

————. *Leaving Home*. Levittown, PA: Brunner/Mazel, Inc., 1997.

Haley, Jay, ed. *Advanced Techniques of Hypnosis and Therapy—Selected Papers of Milton H. Erickson, M.D.* New York: Grune & Stratton, 1967.

Halverson, Andrea M., Mark Hallahan, Allen J. Hart, and Robert Rosenthal. "Reducing the Biasing Effects of Judges' Nonverbal Behavior with Simplified Jury Instruction." *Journal of Applied Psychology* 82, no. 4 (1997): 590-98.

Jung, Carl Gustav. *The Portable Jung*. New York: Viking Press, 1971.

Keim, James, and Madanes, Cloé. Personal communication. 2003.

Lacan, Jacques. *The Four Fundamental Concepts of Psycho-Analysis*. New York: W.W. Norton & Company, 1981.

Laing, Ronald D. *The Politics of the Family and Other Essays*. New York: Pantheon Books, 1971.

Lederer, William, and Don D. Jackson. *The Mirages of Marriage*. New York: Norton, 1968.

LeDoux, Joseph. *The Emotional Brain: The Mysterious Underpinnings of Emotional Life*. New York: Touchstone Books, 1998.

Madanes, Cloé. *Strategic Family Therapy.* San Francisco: Jossey-Bass, 1981.

———. *Behind the One-Way Mirror—Advances in the Practice of Strategic Therapy.* San Francisco: Jossey-Bass, 1984.

———. *Sex, Love, and Violence—Strategies for Transformation.* New York: Norton, 1990.

———. *The Secret Meaning of Money.* San Francisco: Jossey-Bass, 1994.

———. *The Violence of Men.* San Francisco: Jossey-Bass, 1995.

———. "Remembering Our Heritage." *Psychotherapy Networker,* Nov.-Dec. 2004.

———. *The Therapist As Humanist, Social Activist and Systemic Thinker . . . And Other Selected Papers.* Phoenix, AZ: Zeig, Tucker, and Theisen, 2006.

Peysha, Mark, and Cloé Madanes. *Action Book* for the film *Back From the Edge.* La Jolla, CA: Robbins-Madanes Center for Strategic Intervention, 2004.

———. *Action Book* for the film *Conquering Overwhelming Loss: Rediscovering a Compelling Future.* La Jolla, CA: Robbins-Madanes Center for Strategic Intervention, 2004.

———. *Action Book* for the film *Negotiating Conflict: Leadership in Times of Crisis.* La Jolla, CA: Robbins-Madanes Center for Strategic Intervention, 2004.

———. *Action Book* for the film *Reclaiming Your True Identity: The Power of Vulnerability.* La Jolla, CA: Robbins-Madanes Center for Strategic Intervention, 2004.

Robbins, A. *Awaken the Giant Within.* New York: Simon & Schuster, 1991.

Robbins, Anthony, and Cloé Madanes. *Back from the Edge.* A film from the Robbins-Madanes Center for Strategic Intervention, 2005.

———. *Conquering Overwhelming Loss: Rediscovering a Compelling Future.* A film from the Robbins-Madanes Center for Strategic Intervention, 2004.

———. *Negotiating Conflict: Leadership in Times of Crisis.* A film from the Robbins-Madanes Center for Strategic Intervention, 2004.

———. *Reclaiming Your True Identity: The Power of Vulnerability.* A film from the Robbins-Madanes Center for Strategic Intervention, 2004.

Rosenthal, Robert. *Judgment Studies: Design, Analysis, and Meta-Analysis.* New York: Cambridge University Press, 1987.

Rosenthal, Robert, and Lenore Jacobson. *Pygmalion in the Classroom.* Expanded edition. New York: Irvington, 1992.

Schneirla, Theodore C., and Gerard Piel. "The Army Ant." *Twentieth-Century Bestiary.* By the editors of *Scientific American.* New York: Simon & Schuster, 1955.

Schultz, Wolfram. "Getting Formal with Dopamine and Reward." *Neuron* 36 (2002): 241-63.

Seligman, Martin. *Learned Optimism.* New York: Alfred A. Knopf, Inc., 1991.

Siegel, Daniel. *The Developing Mind: How Relationships and the Brain Interact to Shape Who We Are.* New York: Guilford Press, 1999.

Thomas, Lewis. *The Medusa and the Snail.* New York: Bantam Books, 1980.

Volk, Tyler. *Metapatterns—Across Space, Time, and Mind.* New York: Columbia University Press, 1995.

Watzlawick, Paul. *How Real Is Real? Confusion, Disinformation, Communication.* New York: Norton, 1976.

———. "'Insight' May Cause Blindness." *The Evolution of Psychotherapy—The Third Conference.* Ed. Jeffrey Zeig. New York: Brunner/Mazel, Inc., 1997.

Zweig, Jason. "Are You Wired for Wealth?" *Money,* October, 2002. http://money.cnn.com/magazines/moneymag/moneymag_archive/2002/10/01/328637/index.htm

INDEX

———— //////////////////////////// ————

A

Action
    acting and, 17
    benefits of, visualizing, 92, 98–99
    choice and, 16
    conditioning new, 110–11
    taking specific, 92, 98–99
Agreement
    direct, 152
    indirect, 151
Alternation, 34
Alternatives, creating new
    empowering, 109–10
Analogue communication, 65–66
Anderson, Steve, 10
Apologizing, 97–98
Appreciation, 29–30, 98.
    See also Gratitude
Archetypes, 105–7, 155
Association, 35
Attachment disorder, 15

B

Bateson, Gregory, 57
Bavelas, Alex, 32–33, 50
Behavior
    changing, 36, 92–93
    symmetrical, 57–58

Beliefs
    breakthrough relationships and,
        153–54
    challenging limiting, 88, 93–94
    change and, 87
    core, 32–37
    defining, 155
    developing, 32–36
    helplessness and patterns causing,
        121
    limiting, 32
    need for, 32–33
    relationships and, 87
    self-love and, 36–37
    superstitions and, 33–34, 36
Benefits of action, visualizing, 92, 98–99
Bennis, Warren, 50
Body and change, 145–46
Breakthrough relationships
    beliefs and, 153–54
    case studies
        focusing on father, 112–13
        love, 113–15
        novel solution, 115–19
    notes, 215–21
    steps to
        condition new thought/
            emotion/decision/action,
            110–11

Breakthrough relationships
    beliefs and,
    steps to (*cont*)
        define problem in solvable
            terms, 108–9
        get leverage, 104–7
        interrupt limiting/destructive
            habitual patterns, 107–8
        relate to a higher purpose or
            connect to empowering
            environment, 111
        understand your and other
            person's model world, 101–4
    terminology, 155–59
    workbook, 161–214
Breiter, Hans, 35

C

Caplow, Theodore, 50
Certainty/comfort need, 19–20, 22
Chain organizational model, 50
Change
    behavioral, 36, 92–93
    beliefs and, 87
    body and, 145–46
    committing to, 89–90, 96
    conflict and, 107
    desired, 12–14
    emotional, 46–47
    of focus, 5–6, 8, 14
    identity and, 92–93
    self-identity and, 92–93
    strategy for, 131–32
Choice, 16
Circle organizational model, 50
Circles, 49–51
Commitment, 89–90, 96
Communication
    analogue, 65–66
    conflict and, 67–68
    depression and, 71
    digital, 65–66
    direct, 150

expectations and, 78–80
importance of, 65
indirect, 156–57
irrational aspects of relationships
    and, 71–73
meaning and, 66–67
metaphoric, 68–70
operations used to induce others,
    81–83
paradoxical, 70
sequence of interaction and, 66–70
sexual, 69–71
straightforward, 70
types of, 65
weapons
    criticism, 73–74
    generosity, 74–75
    indirect influence, 75–76
    induction, 76–77
    negative projection, 77–78
    sarcasm, 73
Compassion, 16
Conditioning new thoughts/emotions/
    decision/action, 110–11
Conflict
    change and, 107
    communication and, 67–68
    defining, 155
    habitual mode of, changing, 5–6
    of values, 42–43
Context, setting, 98
Contribution need, 21–23
Core beliefs, 32–37
Criticism, 73–74
Cross-generational coalitions,
    52–55

D

Darwin, Charles, 6
Death. *See* Loss
Decisions
    conditioning new, 110–11
    indirect influence on, 75–76

key
    apologizing for hurtful, 97–98
    connecting to consequences of, 89, 95–96
    consequences of, 37-38
    defining, 157
    discovering and understanding, 89, 94–95
    in model of world, 37-40
    qualities of powerful, 38–39
Denial, 81
Depression, 71
Despair
    benefits of, 140–43
    defining, 155–56
Digital communication, 65–66
Direct agreement, 152
Direct communication, 150
Displacement, 81
Dopamine, 35
Drives, basic, 15
Dyads, 49

E

Emotional resources, building up, 90, 96–97
Emotional states repeatedly experienced, 44–47
Emotions
    case study, 46–47
    changing, 46–47
    conditioning new, 110–11
    controlling, 44–45
    defining, 156
    as driving forces, 44
    influences on, 46
    meaning of life and, 46
    mental functions and, 46
    physiology and, 98
    September 11, 2001, terrorist attacks and, 45–46
    steps regulating thinking and behavior, 45

Environment, connecting to empowering, 111
Expectations
    communication and, 78–80
    power of, 78–80
    raising, 80

F

Father-son coalition, 55
Fears, primary, 26–27
Focus
    change of, 5–6, 8, 14
    importance of, 159
Forecasting, 34–35
Freud, Sigmund, 6, 15
Future
    creating compelling
        case study, 146–48
        defining true purpose, 143–44
        evaluating initial response, 141–42
        finding multiple ways to achieve purpose, 144
        identifying needs to be satisfied, 142
        loss and, 146
        overview, 140–41
        process, 146
        resolutions and, beyond, 257
        understanding side benefits of being in despair, 142–43
        using body to create change in self, 145–46
    defining, 156

G

Generosity, 74–75
Gratitude, 156. *See also* Appreciation
Growth need, 21, 23

H

Habitual patterns, interrupting limiting/destructive, 107–8

Habitual questions asked of self, 43–44

Headache, literal and metaphoric, 123–25

Helplessness
    belief patterns causing, 121
    case studies
        drop dead, witch, 132–34
        headache, literal and metaphoric, 123–25
        strategy for change, 131–32
        wicked stepmother, 125–31
    defining, 156
    power and, 122–23
    strategy for change and, 131–32

Hierarchies and power
    circles, 49–51
    cross-generational coalitions, 52–55
    dyads, 49
    father-son coalition, 55
    incongruity and, 56
    in marriage, 53
    meaning and, 67
    mother-child coalition, 54–55
    networks, 62–64
    passion and, relighting, 60–61
    peers, 51–52
    power struggles, 56–60
    symmetrical relationships, 56–60
    triads, 50
    triangles, 49–51, 158

Huettel, Scott, 34–35

Human needs psychology, 16–17

Hypnosis, 75–76

I

Identification, 82

Identity
    challenge limiting, 88, 93–94
    change and, 92–93
    giving up old, 39–40
    steps for reclaiming true
        build up emotional resources, 90–91, 96–97
        case study, 87–92
        challenge limiting beliefs and identity, 88, 93–94
        commit to changing, 89–90, 96
        connect to consequences of key decisions, 89, 95–96
        discover and understand key decisions, 89, 94–95
        strategize ways to reclaim identity, 91, 97–98
        take specific action and visualize benefits, 92, 98–99

I feeling, 3

Incongruity, 56

Indirect agreement, 151

Indirect communication, 156–57

Indirect influence, 75–76

Indirect negotiation. See Negotiation, indirect

Individual. See also Self-identity
    as cause of problems, 4–5
    clarifying question about, 148–49
    identity of
        change and, 92–93
        giving up old, 39–40
    question, clarifying, 148–49

Induction
    operations of, 81–83
    as weapon of communication, 76–77

Instincts, 15

Interaction, sequence of, 66–70

Introjection, 82

J

Joy, 157

K

Key decisions. *See* Decisions
Kim, Irene, 35

L

Leverage, getting, 104–7
Life, metaphors for, 32
Life cycle, 27–30, 157
Listening, 151
Loss
    benefits of sadness/despair and,
      140–43
    case studies, 138–40, 146–48
    future and, creating compelling
      case study, 146–48
      defining true purpose,
        143–44
      evaluating initial response,
        141–42
      finding multiple ways to achieve
        purpose, 144
      identifying needs to be satisfied,
        142
      loss and 146
      overview, 140–41
      process of, 146
      resolutions and, beyond,
        257
      understanding side benefits of
        being in despair, 142–43
      using body to create change in
        self, 145
    inevitability of, 135
    memory and, recovering lost,
      136–38
    mourning and, importance of,
      135–36
    resolutions and, beyond, 148
Love, everlasting, key to, 27
Love/connection need, 21, 23,
    26
Lover archetype, 106

M

Magician archetype, 105–6
Malignant escalation, 157
Marriage. *See also* Relationships
    complementary, 57
    hierarchies in, 53
    power in, 53
    power struggle in, 58–59
Meaning
    communication and, 66–67
    hierarchy and, 67
    of life, 46
Memories, creating good, 10–12
Meta-frame, 150–51
Metaphoric communication, 68–70
Mimosa girdler beetle, 13–14
Model of world
    beliefs, core, 32–37
    decisions, key, 37–40
    defining, 31
    emotional states repeatedly
      experienced, 44–47
    habitual questions asked of self,
      43–44
    negative results from personal,
      47–48
    positive results from personal,
      47–48
    references, personal, 43
    understanding own and other
      person's, 101–4
    values, life, 40–43
Mother-child coalition, 54–55
Mourning, 135–36. *See also* Loss
Mystification, 82–83

N

Needs
    basic
      certainty/comfort, 19–20, 22
      contribution, 21–23
      growth, 21, 23

Needs
  basic (*cont*)
    love/connection, 21, 23, 26
    significance, 20–23, 26–27
    uncertainty/variety, 20, 22, 26
  for beliefs, 32–33
  case studies, 23–27, 29–30
  defining, 157
  human needs psychology and, 16–17
  identifying two primary, 24–27
  life cycle and, 27–30
  love and, everlasting, 27
  relationships and, 4
  satisfying, 22–23, 27, 142
Negative projection, 77–78
Negotiation, indirect
  clarify individual question, 148–49
  direct agreement, 152
  do not communicate directly, 150
  indirect agreement, 151
  listen and take notes, 151
Networks, power of, 62–64
Notes, taking, 151

helplessness and, 122–23
in marriage, 53
of networks, 62–64
of peers, 51–52
struggles, 56–60
Precedents, 38–39
Priorities, 26
Problems
  attempted solutions for
    as bigger problem, 7–9
    changing, 9
    in sustaining problem, 6–7
  change desired and, 12–14
  defining, 108–9
  individual as cause of, 4–5
  memories and, creating good,
    10–12
Projection, 77–78, 82
Psychology, 15–16
Purpose
  achieving, 144
  defining true, 143–44
  relating to higher, 111

O

Organizational models, 50–51
Organizations, 157–58

P

Pain, raising level of, 104–5
Paradoxical communication, 70
Passion, relighting, 60–61
Patterns, 158
Pavlov, Ivan, 35
Peers, 51–52
Physiology and emotions, 98
Point of view, 67
Posture, 145–46
Power. *See also* Hierarchies and power
  cross-generational, 52–55
  of expectations, 78–80

Q

Questions
  clarifying individual, 148–49
  regularly asked, 158

R

Rationalization, 82
References, personal, 43
Regression, 82
Regret, expressing, 97–98
Relationships. *See also* Breakthrough
  relationships; Marriage
  appreciation in, 29–30
  beliefs and, 87
  irrational aspects of, 71–73
  life cycle of, 27–30
  needs and, 4

plan for, 12–14
power struggles in, 56–60
symmetrical, 56–60
troubled, transforming, 3–4
understanding, 4
We feeling of, 3
work involved in good, 3–4
Repetition, 34, 39, 69–70
Repetition compulsion, 6
Replacement, 81–82
Repression, 82
Respect, 16
Response, evaluating initial, 141–42
Responsibility, 16, 158
Reversal, 83
Reward, 39
Robbins, Anthony (Tony), 45, 87–92
Rosenthal, Robert, 78–79

S

Sadness, benefits of, 140
Sarcasm, 73
Schultz, Wolfram, 35
Scotomatization, 81
Self-determination, 16, 158
Self-identity
    change and, 92–93
    giving up old, 39–40
    steps for reclaiming true
        build up emotional resources,
            90–91, 96–97
        case study, 87–92
        challenge limiting beliefs and
            identity, 88, 93–94
        commit to changing, 89–90, 96
        connect to consequences of key
            decisions, 89, 95–96
        discover and understand key
            decisions, 89, 94–95
        strategize ways to reclaim
            identity, 91, 97–98
        take specific action and
            visualize benefits, 92, 98–99

Self-love, 36–37
Seligman, Martin, 121
Sequence of interaction, 66–70
Sexual communication, 69–71
Significance need, 20–23, 26–27
Sisters, 63
Solutions to problems, attempted
    as bigger problem, 7–9
    changing, 9
    in sustaining problem, 6–7
Sovereign archetype, 106
Split personalities, 83
Status differences, 13
Straightforward communication, 70
Strategizing, 91, 97–98
Superstitions, 33–34, 36
Symmetrical behavior, 57–58
Symmetrical relationships, 56–60
Systems thinking, 15–16

T

Taking notes, 151
Thomas, Lewis, 12–14
Thoughts, conditioning new, 110–11
Triads, 50
Triangles, 49–51, 158

U

Uncertainty/variety need, 20, 22, 26
Unit of one point of view, 67
Unit of three point of view, 67
Unit of two point of view, 67

V

Values
    conflict of, 42–43
    life, 40–43
    underlying, 159
Vehicles, 159

W

Warrior archetype, 105
Waste, 159
Watzlawick, Paul, 34
We feeling, 3
Wheel organizational model, 50
Workbook, 161–214

X

Xemplary life, 159

Y

You, 159

Z

Zero in, 159. *See also* Focus